ANCHOR BOOKS

IN FROM THE COLD

Edited by

David Foskett

First published in Great Britain in 1996 by
ANCHOR BOOKS
1-2 Wainman Road, Woodston,
Peterborough, PE2 7BU

HB ISBN 1 85930 381 1
SB ISBN 1 85930 386 2

Foreword

Anchor Books is a small press, established in 1992, with the aim of promoting readable poetry to as wide an audience as possible.

We hope to establish an out for writers of poetry who may have struggled to see their work in print.

The poems presented here have been selected from many entries. Editing proved to be a difficult and daunting task and as the Editor, the final selection was mine.

'In From The Cold' is a very special anthology which has been produced in association with Wood Green Animal Shelter, along with the support and quality work submitted by the animal loving poets included.

Just by looking at the variety of poetry included in this special anthology, you can tell we are a nation of animal loves. Although cats and dogs take the main spotlight, throughout the book there are still many other pets that are well looked after and loved by the general public like yourself.

As royalties from this book will be donated to WGAS, we must not forget the hard work and dedication these people put into their work to ensure neglected animals get nursed back to good health and find a fun-loving family like all the families included here. Let's not forget animals are for life, not just for Christmas.

I trust this selection will delight and please the authors and all those who enjoy reading poetry.

David Foskett
Editor

CONTENTS

GUINNESS

Named after an Irish stout;
Some white, black most part.
Of faithful heart there's no doubt;
Quick to steal your heart.

My heart, he stole, at first sight;
A fluffy black ball;
Almost hidden by grass height;
Soon loved by us all.

Lived as one of family,
Plans included him.
Watched our each move craftily,
Knew every whim.

Each look of expectation;
Nuzzle at your knee;
Seeking some delectation
With each artful plea.

Happy running off the lead,
Sniffing as he went;
Sometimes your call he would heed,
If not strong, the scent.

He was happy to the end;
But now age has won;
We've said farewell to our friend,
His job on earth done.

He showed his love without speech;
Message he does give -
For others' hearts you can reach
By way that you live.

Roy Hammond

KINDRED SPIRITS

Joyful whinnies of affection shatter early morning peace,
As the stable lads approach their hungry steeds.
Swapping soiled stalls for sunlit yard, they squeal at sweet release,
Whilst the faithful grooms attend their every needs.

In a tree-lined field across the way, two legendary giants meet,
Big Alec drops a bale of hay, beside the huge black stallion's feet.
The tall tanned foreman's callused hands caress the gleaming silken coat,
Whilst like a statue Samson stands, deep moans erupting from his throat.

That memorable encounter, when the two free souls first met,
Was the subject for discussion in the little Clydeside town.
Summoned from his evening leisure, by a wild-eyed trembling vet,
Alec quickly intervened when told a horse could be put down.

Defying every effort to unload him from the van,
The kicking screaming animal was eventually sedated.
With painful self-inflicted wounds from which the horse's blood still ran,
The unbowed warrior bared his teeth, as Alec calmly watched and waited.

Left alone behind locked gates, the long tense staring duel began,
Portraying all that Samson hates, Alec starts his bonding plan.
Aware the stallion did not feed since rescued from his war-torn hell,
Alec knows what he will need to make the suffering orphan well.

Pangs of hunger and sweet carrots tempted Samson to submit,
With deadly jaws diverted, Alec used his magic touch.
Gently spraying soothing lotion which would help the cuts to knit,
His soft brogue builds a friendship that would come to mean so much.

Frank Smiley

THE OTTER

Playful, joyful, noisy, bright.
The otter is a sheer delight.
Mischievous in every way,
Out at night, sleeps by day.
In a holt, under a tree.
Out of sight from you or me.
In the river, quick and smart,
After fish she'll swiftly dart.
Catching one or two, or more,
Then she takes them to the shore,
To eat at leisure, with sheer pleasure.
She's smooth and sleek,
We must protect her.
From man she must hide.
Waiting for the river's tide,
To take her to the sea.

Sandra Houghton

PETS

A pet brings us joy
When we grow old
Something to love in this sad old world
When we're not as busy as we used to be
A kitten brings pleasure sat on our knee
A puppy will get us out for a walk
A parrot will sit in his cage and talk
A canary will sing us a lovely old song
And the days pass quickly
Not half as long.

J Floyd

3

BLACKBIRD

O blackbird of the golden beak,
Land lightly 'neath my sill,
And sing a favourite song beneath
With notes that through me thrill.

Tip the tail there as you touch,
Tip the tail and search,
Morning's light does promise much
For birds down from the perch.

And in th' evening's quiet hours
Flitter through the grass,
Amid the wild and garden flowers
That touch you as you pass.

O blackbird of the golden beak,
Where does your lady fly?
Follow her, her warm nest seek,
And rest your roving eye.

Into the wood I watch him fly,
Through the leafy dark,
The bird of golden-ringlet eye;
His lulling flight I mark.

And I wonder where he goes,
How far, how deep within,
Through shades the moonlight never knows
And dappled starlight's glim.

David A Hall

SOULMATE

I remember the day I visited Battersea Dogs Home
There you sat in a kennel frightened and all alone
Although there were hundreds of dogs to see
Instantly I knew you were the one for me
Terrified and all of a quiver
Your poor little body did nothing but shiver
I bent down and held out my hand
But it was all you could do to stand
You came over to me after a while
My heart melted and I began to smile
Later that day I took you home
And promised you never again would you be alone
To care and love you I knew I must
I had to work hard to gain your trust
Soon the day came when you were jumping for joy
You'd go mad playing with your favourite toy
At night when you began to tire
You'd snuggle up at my feet in front of the fire
Your coat was all shiny and bright
I'd let you sleep at the end of my bed each night
Out in the front garden I would let you play
If only I hadn't on that particular day
As soon as I heard the car brakes slam
Out into the street I ran
When I reached you I knew I was too late
In you I have lost my soulmate
With each day that passes by
My eyes fill with tears and I begin to cry
You felt no pain of that I'm sure
My beloved dog Bobby you need be frightened no more.

Marion Evans

A SUPERSTAR
MADE IN HEAVEN

'But, it was only a cat!'
No dear Dean, you were more than that.
You were an acrobat, our sobriquet 'Little Chap'.
There was no one dafter.
Two years of love, joy and laughter
Embracing us ever after, each day a brand new chapter.

You'd view your world upside down
From under a rug, to play the clown.
Even at the window peering in,
With show jump skills you'd come flying in.
Or by the door, waiting there,
First light at dawn, to 'nose the air'.
The great outdoors was yours to claim,
You loved your freedom, a constant game.

Memories of a bright-eyed star
Just chasing leaves, in the path of a car,
Which was to permanently bar
Your boundless energy; too young to mar.
Lifeless limbs, sightless eyes,
Cuddled and kissed with anguished cries -
Alas no more would you respond in kind -
Reasoning lies, when a loved one dies.

Now our emotions are hard to bear.
Your ghost is everywhere; a ball upon the stair,
A dented cushion, coated with your hair,
Lonely Torvill's on your empty chair -
We buried you 'neath your garden lair,
We wanted you near, for we still care.

Jenny Wright

BATTERSEA PUPPIES

Oh he's so cute and so is she,
What size would the furry one grow to be,
Please pick me, I need a home,
I want to run and jump and roam,
I'll take him *Sir*, does he mean *me?*
This ain't no life in Battersea,
He's not for Christmas, he's for life,
I know that *Sir*, he's for my wife,
She'll spoil him in every way,
I'll take him to the park each day,
My first bark was gentle and sweet,
As I stood at my master's feet,
And now there's good food in my dish,
Instead of dog food I get fish,
He even takes me to the park,
I make sure he's safe when it's dark,
Now there's a roof above my head,
And each day I know I'll be fed,
Thank you Master for my toy,
This puppy here's a happy boy,
I'll bring hours of endless fun,
If you pick me, the furry one,
I still feel sad when you go away,
But you come back to me each day,
Bringing buttons, bringing food,
I love you Master, you're real good.

Alan Thomson

LOVED ANIMAL

I feel I would like to contribute for the *WGAS*
With saying, we owned a golden Labrador, until the age of 13 years plus,
She was obedient, so gentle and lovely,
Her name was adorable unforgettable Libby,
We owned her when she was at the age of 18 months old,
At first, she did run away, perhaps to try to find her real master, so we were
                                                                told,
When we did at last find her, her paws were red and raw, and sore,
After bathing and putting ointment on them, she never ran away any more,
We loved her, as she loved us, until old age crept along,
Until she died peacefully while I was holding her, at that time when we knew
                                                something was wrong,
I will never forget the time when walking her, she picked up a stray bone in
                                                the street,
I took it away from her mouth, and threw it a couple of feet,
Even at her old age, she sulked that night for hours on end,
Her ears stood up, when we told her not to fret, that dear old friend,
I told her, next day I will get her some more,
When we walked to the shop that day to get her fresh bones at the butcher's
                                                store,
She just wanted the lot, when I told her this won't do,
Her ears still stood up, but she was contented when she only had two,
All animals have senses, dogs are good when they are trained properly,
Animal owners, from the beginning should be firm but kind, then a friend
                                                you will see,
Whether they are crossbreeds, Border, collies, even to the boxer,
Even if they are sloppy, fierce-looking, but gentle, you just have to adore,
Sue, a Border collie we possessed, when at earlier days,
She would follow us everywhere, so loyal in her ways,
Long walks, short walks, the favourite of course was the park,
Even to go for a swim in the summer, before it got dark,
Shaking, herself until she got dry,
Until dusk arrived through the cloudless sky,

Homeward bound, tired but happy we were, and just walking slow,
Dog biscuits were deserved, animals always seem to know,
All animal owners, treat animals with kindness, and talk to them, they will be
your friend,
Until they retire in restful sleep, right to the end.

Jean P McGovern

JUDY

Bright summer days without diminish
Feeling the warmth of invisible rays of light.
Games that partook our all without finish
Friendship that burned forever so bright.
These are thoughts that have become fewer yet never wrong,
As the years have grown and moved us apart.
Yet the temper of their steel is forever strong,
And plunges deep into the depths of my heart.
To have had a friend so faithful, and true,
Was a blessing that enriched me in my younger days.
And so the parting when it came, because of you,
Made one understand, that for such, someone always pays.
We couldn't keep you as we had to move to our new home
My Judy was to go for her own good to a farm
My dog, my companion with whom I would no longer roam,
For her good went and I suffered untold harm.
To love is to give of yourself through and through,
To share and to feel never two but always one
And to lose such love is to lose part of you
The whole is bettered when the parts produce the sum.

David G Moore

FEELING THEIR AGE

Come play with me. Come play with me
Mewed Bubbles with a pat of his paw.
So gently to old 'Paddy'.
Whose look made the kitten withdraw.

Come play with me, he cried again
As he jumped and frisked to and fro.
Behave yourself, be quiet!
You are new here, I'll have you know.

Then big black 'Charlie' (from next door)
Came to see what was going on,
He flicked his tail with great disdain
And said, 'Playing is just not on.'

The cats sat on their dignity
Viewed Bubbles with sardonic eye.
Yet it wasn't very long ago
That they were young and spry.

Vera Raymond

A DOGGY STORY

He sniffs around the old dustbins
Eating out in yards from tins
His coat is shaggy wants a wash
Across the yard he makes a dash,
He comes close you talk to him
And feel his bones he's very thin
He licks your hand, those mournful eyes
Please take me home, they gently cry
Who could desert a dog like this?
A loving friend, I'm sure they'll miss.

Thelma Hynes

WATER BABIES

Never a sound
never a smile
round and round they go

Green, gold, blue
humourless eyes
stare unblinkingly through glass

Jaws sag open
mouths feeble men
mirthless, monotonous faces

Dogfish steer
graceful zeppelins
in and out of their domain

shoal silver fish
silver grey blimps
hesitating in mid-water

baleful, bulging
green/blue eye
unfolding a tentacle or two

closed umbrella
with no handle
without bones/blood/flesh

he cranes
withered neck
forward, spreads his toes

pushing himself
upwards towards
hand that feeds him

Teresa Webster

11

JERRY V BENNY

Jerry one
became
Jerry four!
Each one loved even more . . .
than the last.

Please do not drop
him on the floor.

Benny our dog,
loves Jerry . . .
for tea!
Strawjerry jam!
That's his plan.

Phoebe said to me,
'Hamsters are fairies' horses'
I said,
'More like fairies' buffalo!'

We smiled into each other's eyes.
Jerry, well - yes,
he's very much alive.

That is
until Jerry four
became
Jerry five . . .

Cora Tanner

MINKIE

Humility fills your soul,
and love your heart.
Your deep brown velvet eyes
sparkle with the joy of living.
Lithe of limb -
slender as a willow wand,
you run like the wind,
enjoying the freedom of play.
A shy, affectionate
mini dachshund,
whose adoration knows no bounds.

Elizabeth Robertson

POWERFUL FELINE

You can watch and be amazed,
At the speed a feline can run,
Its dark spotty fawn coat,
That shines so colourful in the sun,
His large powerful legs,
Pound so graceful on the ground,
Leaving the air,
Whirlwind all around.

A leopard is so strong,
And yet so bold,
His face can be motionless,
With stories untold,
Only his prey can be caught,
After a dramatic chase,
Remembering not to turn back,
For a look in his face.

Mary-Ann Adams

FAITHFUL FRIENDS

Here we sit my dogs and me
Relaxing on our large settee
Which once was filled with loads of toys
Children's laughter, the girls and boys.

Then one day I looked around
The house was empty, not a sound,
No more children, for they had grown
With lives to live, had all left home.

But two Chihuahuas, one dark, one red
Share my home and share my bed.
Big dark eyes, both have long hair.
I'm never lonely when they are there.

A favourite hobby of which they're fond
Is to lie and watch my garden pond.
Waiting for a prowling cat
To snatch the frogs from whence they sat.

Like bullets from a loaded gun
'After them, oh! This is fun.'
And the cats keep coming every day
Even though they're chased away.

Whether cats or prowlers, light or dark
The slightest noise and they will bark.
They may be small and lack the height
But in the ankles they will bite.

They're so devoted, lots of fun,
A mad half hour, back and forth they run.
Through the kitchen and up the stairs
Under tables and over chairs.

Faithful friends they'll always be
For I feel safe when they're with me.

M Sievwright

MY BLACK CAT KITSIE

Jet black fur and eyes of gold,
Star of white on chest so bold;
My lovely, cuddly, silky cat
Waits patiently upon the mat.

He welcomes me from treks afar
And peers around the door ajar,
Always singing, always bright,
Oh he is a happy sight!

Purring, rolling on my feet,
Such affection me to greet;
Marching with his outstretched paws
On the spot, without a pause!

Waiting for his steaming fish
As it cools upon the dish
Slowly then his head he dips
And eagerly he licks his lips.

Satisfied and duly fed
He searches for a comfy bed;
Looks at table, looks at chair
Decides, it really can't be there.

He snuggles down then for his nap
Warm as toast upon my lap,
Soft and cosy, full of love,
Singing softly, like a dove.

Contented, happy, furry, ritzy
This is my - black cat -Kitsie!

Mollie D Earl

COUNTRY COMPANIONS

Me and my dog go walking for miles
We walk across fields and I climb over stiles
My dog squeezes under the stiles after me
We go into the woodland to inspect the country.

Wild rabbits and birds scatter as we pass by
And as beauty surrounds me my dog chases a fly
A squirrel boldly runs across my path
His swiftness and antics make me laugh.

We continue our journey through the trees
Now walking in bluebells up to my knees
Clumps of yellow primrose mixed in with the blue
What nice flowers with pretty colours, I might pick a few.

My dog starts to bark she wants to go on her way
There is plenty of time I have got all day
But I leave the flowers, she will not let me pick
My dog is running ahead and has now found a stick.

I meet up with some ramblers on a nature walk
They stop for a while and we have a talk
We talk about the beauty that is all around
Then my dog comes back to see what I have found.

She barks at the strangers, who are not amused
My dog looks at me a little confused
She wants a fuss or maybe a pat
But strangers do not do things like that.

As we turn to go home my dog and me
She runs on ahead and once more sniffs a tree
I would never give up my country life
For life in a city, full of trouble and strife.

Brenda Colvin

ALL OUR LITTLE ANIMALS

Please be kind and don't be cruel
To the animals we love,
Who came to us on Noah's Ark,
They were sent by God above.
They bring us lots of joy
When our lives are in a muddle,
They are always there to pick up to love and hug and cuddle.
They are very different from humans,
You can trust them all you see.
They will never let us down,
They are good for you and me.
I really love our animals,
I really really do.
I'm glad God sent our animals
To be here for me and you.

Alexander Roberston

BORIS

He sauntered up the garden path
Dejected, sad and thin,
His pleading eyes seemed to say
Please, please take me in.
His fluffy coat was matted,
He was all alone and lost.
I couldn't turn him from my door
No matter what it cost
I stooped and stroked his weary head
The purrs came thick and fast
His wandering days were over
He'd found a friend at last

Betty Jane Shanks

MY LITTLE DOG CALLED PRECIOUS

My little dog called Precious,
Means everything to me.
Because she is a lovely dog,
As everyone can see.

She has her funny moments too,
But then so do we all,
But one thing I like about her,
She answers my every call.

I put her bowl on the floor,
With all her dinner in.
But do you think that she will eat it?
No that's just another thing.

She has her little bean bag,
Which she lays in all the time,
But when we have a cup of tea,
Her eyes are fixed on mine.

I've never seen a dog quite like her.
She really likes her cup of tea,
And with her little mug beside her,
She thinks she's just like me.

She has a funny name I know,
But Precious she is to me.
I don't think that I could ever change her,
As how heartless could I be?

J A Ledger

THE MOUSE

At the dead of night when all are asleep
Out from his hole the little mouse creeps.
He scampers and scurries and slides on the floor,
He's making his way to the back kitchen door
Climbing in cupboards in a determined mood
This mouse is hungry, he's looking for food.
What shall he taste first, the cake or the bread?
He'd better be careful lest he bang his head.
This cake doesn't taste nice he thinks to himself
He'd better try further up on the shelf.
Yes, that's what he's after a big piece of cheese,
The taste and the smell, are making him sneeze
He nibbles and nibbles till he's ate it all
Better be careful mouse you're going to fall.
Now his meal's finished he looks for a drink
Gently but swiftly he climbs in the sink.
There he finds water to wash down the cheese
Lapping the water, he feels very pleased.
That was a good night's work one he'll repeat
Tomorrow night when all the house is asleep.
But for the moment he's happy to make his way home
To the hole in the skirting, where he lives all alone.
Now if you ever see him, don't scare him away,
For he's pretty harmless in a roundabout way
He's classed as a menace, he's classed as a pest
But he's one of God's creatures just like the rest.
So don't catch him, or kill him, or leave him to die
He's as much right to be here, as you have or I
Instead try understanding the life of a mouse,
Who lives under the floorboards in many a house.

Dorothy Cirillo

POPPY

Nanna has a little dog and Poppy is her name
She's a Yorkie, full of fun and ready for a game
There's a basket where she sleeps and another for her toys
And when she's in a playful mood Poppy comes to us two boys.

A ball of wool she brings for us to tug and play
Then pouncing on a squeaky toy she'll suddenly dash away
So it's round the room for a game of chase
And off she goes at such a pace.

When Poppy's tired herself with play
Off to her basket she's away
The blanket's pulled to a lumpy heap
Before she settles down to sleep.

Out for a walk she gaily trots
There are of course occasional stops
In her mouth she holds a glove
She's a charming pet our little love.

Nanna's house is miles away
Oh! What joy when they come to stay
But alas their visit soon must end
And we will miss our little friend.

I am Neil, my brother's Paul, and we're rather sad today
Nanna's going home again so we cheer them on their way
One day soon we'll visit them and delighted Pops will be
She'll rush around with wagging tail and behave excitedly.

M Bowring

BUMBLE - A BLACK CHOW CHOW

A dog he is not wholly
But a bear - in part -
Aloof and distant -
Yet devoted heart.
Unswerving loyalty
Unto the chosen one
Who chose him first
And thus the bond begun.

Slant-eyed and massive
With an ambling gait;
Obedient *always*
(If you care to wait!)
A guard par excellence -
For who would dare
To cross your threshold
When a chow is there?

Eileen Reece

IT'S A DOG'S LIFE

He's got his own dish and his own bed
If I had my way he would sleep in the shed
When out in the car he sits all alone
Always on the front seat, chewing his bone
His meals are served at the same time each day
And he gets quite upset if we're ever away
When watching TV he sits in my chair
I'm beginning to think it's not really fair
His walks are exhausting four miles at a time
They must be completed whether rainy or fine
He's a spaniel by breed and his name is Spot
I must admit it's a dog's life he's got.

Bernard Brazil

NOBODY'S DOG

I am nobody's dog, brought as a Christmas present to a bad family I was sold,
I was a sweet little puppy who got tiresome to hold,
Then one day, when I was older I was thrown out into the cold.
I wish I had a home to go to, I look in other people's windows often,
And see those lucky dogs lying in their baskets of soft cotton,
Or may be on their owners' laps,
Or by the fireside taking their afternoon naps.
I hunt around for scraps for my dinner
And day by day I grow shaggier and thinner
My tail is down and I have a sorry face,
And boy do I hate this place.
I often wish that I could have a home to stay
And a caring owner who will never send me away.

Emma Kemm

FAITHFUL PUP

That little tail keeps wagging,
Much slower now you have grown old.
You still try to bounce like a puppy,
So stubborn you will not be told.
Piercing brown eyes that now have become cloudy,
Shining liver coat that now has turned grey.
Your field-springing days have subsided,
Although you still want us to play.
The years have taken their toll now,
We can see it written in your face.
You once would run like a rabbit,
But now it's a steady pace.
Have I told you today that I love you?
Given you a hug to show you I care?
I wish you could live forever,
Growing old and dying is so unfair.

S Gutteridge

OH TO BE A DOLPHIN ...

Dolphins in the wild, feeling so free;
I wish someone was with them, I wish it was me.
Out in the sea, swimming all around;
Talking to each other, with that wondrous sound.
Oh, to be a dolphin, swimming in the sea;
I wish I was a dolphin, in the sea.
Oh to be a dolphin. Oh yes!
Such beautiful creatures, living in the wild,
If only I could too, but for a while;
Wishing and dreaming, dreaming of the sea;
Be just like a dolphin, so peaceful and, so free ...
There's so much that Man can learn, from these beings from the sea,
The teachings we should take from them, of evolution but,
Do we have the key?
Why are they so beautiful? And, why do they appeal to me so?
Perhaps, one of life's mysteries, that I shall never know?
Swim long and, swim deep, dear princes of the sea;
We shall yearn in awe of you, because you are so free.
Live long the dolphins,
Creators of my dreams ...

Ron Matthews Jr

THE BEJEWELLED

Haughty peacock, bejewelled eyes aglow,
Trembling fan spread beneath the sun,
A shimmering fluorescent show.
Miriad rainbow colours leap and dance
Within this living crescent
Then burst forth to dazzle and entrance.
What in this world can possibly compare
With this beauty offered by God's creature
For me to share?

Paddy Jupp

MY FIRST HORSE

I was scared stiff of horses at first
When I went into the paddock I feared the worst.
Sheba was a horse that liked to be bold.
We practised in the paddock for a few weeks
And then she took me out on the streets.
We went towards Pex Hill down the country lanes
I sat upon Sheba the chestnut with the black mane.
We went along Birchfield Road and on the way home
She took fright and I felt so alone.
The traffic around us all beeped their horns
As Sheba stood upright upon people's lawns.
Away she galloped towards her home
While all around her people did moan.
Another day, we went down Pex Hill Quarry
And that was when I really began to worry.
Could Sheba climb up the gritty sand slopes
Or would she collapse and dash all my hopes?
I needn't have worried, she climbed it with ease
Even though I had gripped her with my knees.
I went home feeling very exhilarated
I could so easily have felt deflated.

June Campbell

PET DUCKS

Though few days old
Their life force prodded ours
Through gimlet eyes
To house, feed and protect.
They grew from thistledown
To cartoon-comics;
He, white, bossy and ample
As though in full sail;
She, brown and neat -
Both graceful in their preen.

So that gimlet-insistence
Made Windermeres
Of sunken troughs;
Mockery of bird-song:
Two 'absurdities'
Who, with rubber beaks
And umbrella feet,
Still one day surprised -
With the architectural
Miracle of an egg!

Herbert Smith

ASPIRING WATCHDOG

They are putting their coats on
I know what that's for,
Soon they will be going out of the door,
They say 'Be good, won't be long.'
But what is long?
I run to the window to watch them go,
What to do next? I don't know.
Lay in my basket, perhaps I'll sleep,
I mustn't think of chasing sheep,
I know that's wrong, because they scold,
Call me to heel, and to do as I'm told.
Get up and stretch, look around,
Something to chew may be found.
An old slipper, a rubber bone,
Wait, they have just come home.
Must bark and make a noise, for you to see,
One day a *watchdog* I will be.

Myrtle Elden

LOUIS

You brought us sunshine, now there's rain
Our lives will never be the same
With a quirky grin and a swish of your tail
Off across the park you'd sail
Dancing in circles, out-running us all
Why didn't you listen to that warning call?
Traffic's a hazard you never could see
So eager to get on the park you would be
Although gone forever, you'll always be there
For dogs like you Louis are ever so rare

Jennifer Moseley

OUR FOUR-LEGGED FRIENDS

How can anyone doubt the love of a dog?
He'll give you his paw, and sits by your side.
He knows your every mood, and
Will nuzzle your hand as if to say,
'Don't be sad I'm here too.'
He will never let you down wherever you go.
He'll guard you, protect you, until it's his time to go.
And all he ever asks of you
Is to give him love and to play.
His eyes follow you, as he lies on the floor.
And you only have to say
'Walkies' and he darts to the door.
You'll never find another friend
So faithful and true to you.
And all because that little word
Called 'love' from me to you.

Alice Polley

FOUR DAYS WITH DAISY

We only had her four short days.
That scruffy ball of love.
A little dog of just two pounds
No longer than a glove.

She really made an impact.
That happy little mite
We picked her up on Thursday.
And she died on Monday night.

How can a little animal.
Impress us in that time?
And take three adult people's lives
Knocking them out of line.

The innocence and loyal trust,
In those little eyes
The delicate proportions
And plaintive little cries.

We felt so lost and helpless,
All we could do was pray.
But someone had decided
She was not meant to stay.

Her short life must have had a purpose
She'll be remembered by these lines.
That most unique of relationships,
Where dog and human intertwines.

T A Napper

OUR DOG

My friend Suki is a greyhound
a lively little bitch
she's really in her element
along the hedge and ditch

She's far too fat to run a race
but she makes the rabbits run
and she does it just to please me
for it's only done for fun

When happy she will wag her tail
when sad looks with doleful eyes
but she's better than most humans
for she never tells me lies

There's a lovely understanding
'tween the teacher and the taught
well it's more than an understanding
it's love that can't be bought

If she can live for fifteen years
and I can do the same
we will have run our race and won
and played the waiting game

She eats the scraps from my table
sometimes sleeps upon my bed
this world would be no place for me
the day that she lies dead

And when at last I stand before my maker
St Peter and his like will toll my bell
I will ask my God to take my dog in His heaven
and gladly pay the cheque way down in hell.

H S Bridge

TWO OF A KIND

A small boy went down to a farmhouse.
There were puppies for sale in a shed.
He found they were far too expensive
So he looked at them playing instead.

How lovely they were as they scampered
And they rolled all around in the straw.
He noticed that one of the puppies
Was quite weak and he had a bad paw.

It seemed to make him more determined
For he chased and he played every game.
The mother loved each of her puppies
And treated them all just the same.

The farmer stood watching the young boy
And said 'He's a cripple, that pup.
He'll never be like all the others
But he's game and he'll never give up.'

The young boy then rolled up his trousers.
Showed a caliper up to his knee.
'I know how that puppy is feeling
For he's lame in his leg just like me.'

'I haven't much money to give you.
Could I please pay you back every week?'
The farmer was very kind hearted
And a tear softly rolled down his cheek.

'My child' said the farmer replying.
'Now I've met you I can't let him stay.
I just know that this puppy will love you.
I want nothing. Please take him away.'

John Christopher Cole

TALES OF A CAT

I'm not the cat who sat on the mat
Not even the one who caught a rat
Don't you dare sit on my chair
Anyway it's full of hair
Creature comforts are what I like
So! Off the chair and on ya bike
I lay here all day content as can be
Dinner at twelve then afternoon tea
I talk to my friends those cute furry mice
I let them have the run of the house
Sometimes I give them a ride on my back
I couldn't harm them, I'm too soft for that
I'm supposed to catch them and throw them out
I'm too sleepy to dash dash about
I sit and read my book till four
Then, my master appears at the door
And I'm poised by the mousehole, oh what a bore
I can hear the mice giggling, somewhere behind
If my master finds out, my death warrant's signed
So I let him think I'm doing my job
So please don't tell him, and I'll give you ten bob.

Sandra Witt

TO CHONG (OUR LOST KITTEN)

You were not of our physical being,
You were not of our creation,
Yet you brought us love and happiness
When into our lives you were born.

Though the time we shared was short,
The memories travel on
For us you are always here
Though for others you are gone.

I do not wish for days gone by
Or treasures I have lost,
For everything we value,
Will stay within our hearts.

So when we think of our ball of fur
With eyes that had no end,
We will realise how lucky we were
To have known our little friend.

Lorraine Ereira

MY LOVE OF CATS

Now I'm living upstairs in a flat
My one regret is that I can't have a cat
Cats and kittens I really adore
And a cat by the fire, I couldn't ask for more
I think of the cats we used to have in family days gone by
Black, tabby and ginger and tabby and white
Each one much loved and bringing delight
There was Timo and Timmy and Ginger Joe
And Candy and wee Willieshwin
Whose owners moved so we took him in
Whiskas was a favourite dish
But sometimes for a treat we gave them fish
I now fill my home with cat things I collect
From china cat figures to tea towels, oven gloves and tray
You name it, I've got it if it has a cat on it.
I can't understand how some people ill treat them
And other animals too
They give us their love and deserve the same back
And are usually a good friend and true
There are other animals I like as well
But my favourite's the cat as I'm sure you can tell.

Shirley Talmadge

I AM JUST A PUSSY CAT

I had a dream
it was not for cream

I wanted to be left at home
so that I can freely roam

I am only a tiny cat
spending my time on a mat

I don't want to be sort
and cunningly caught

taken to a room
full of gloom

with so many men
in that tiny den

with needles and bottles
and a machine that rattles

what am I doing here?
Now I am in fear

I see many of my friends crying
to escape they are trying

It is all such a din
don't they know it is a sin

to cut, and throb and mutilate
when I am so articulate

Humans are supposed to be friendly
but they have proved to be deadly

We look up to them for kindness
and are suffering due to their blindness

They inject us in the name of human health
but it is for sheer greed of wealth

Oh God change the minds of human kind
and make them love us and be kind.

Albert Moses

LIKE JACK

In the early hours of the morning
Is when I go out for a walk,
I never usually see anyone
So I don't even have to talk,
I investigate all the crisp packets
Any bits left inside
If anyone does appear
I scurry away and hide,
4 am still quite dark, try crossing the road,
Here comes a milk-float
With his heavy load,
I freeze till it's gone then run for all I am worth
Into the garden across the way, onto the wet earth
I search amongst the leaves a chocolate wrapper I find
Nearly a quarter of a bar, someone's left behind
So back across the road, wake my kids, sleeping like a log
No I'm not a tramp or a gypsy, but a mother hedgehog
I live near a school, so my lifestyle is great
Lots of goodies dropped near the school gates
Now a single mum, 4 babies to care for, after Jack,
My husband, went out one morning and never came back
Crossing the road, it's quite dangerous is that
Because if a car comes along, we might end up
Quite flat, just,
Like Jack!

Irene Witte

THE FLEDGLING

Little bird hopping near,
So very young you have no fear;
On tiny wings you left the nest
Fluttering down on a venturous quest.

The world around is new to you,
Filled with exciting things to do,
And creepy-crawlies to delight
Your most voracious appetite.

Your parents watch with grave concern,
Knowing how much you have to learn,
Offering a morsel now and then
To teach their offspring how, and when.

Little bird so unconcerned,
Tweeting loud for all to hear,
Does not heed a feline near,
Crouching, ready to spring and pounce,
Gloating in every furry ounce!

Beware! The watching parents shriek
And shake their heads in sad despair,
Fledglings from the nest must learn
All in the garden is not fair.

Lord of the Universe, I pray,
Protect this little one today;
May its wings grow strong, its eyes alert,
That it may fly from tree to tree
Singing praises loud and clear
For all below on earth to hear.

Rose E M Hilham

A DOG'S GAME

Mitzy was a dog,
That was her name,
She was pretty enough,
But acted very strange,
She did have some very
Peculiar ways
She would chase shadows
On walls,
Chew up my golf balls,
And if she heard a cock crow
She would certainly let you know.

Mitzy was a dog,
That was her name,
She liked playing lots of games,
She would bark at bells,
Make cats' lives hell,
And if that wasn't enough,
She liked to roll in cow muck.

Mitzy was a dog,
That was her name,
She liked to bath on hot
Summer days,
She would roll on her back,
And she didn't half yap,
She liked going walks,
And sometimes I swear
She was trying to talk.

Mitzy was a dog,
That was her name,
And I will surely never
Meet another the same,
For life to Mitzy is
Just really a dog's game.

Kevin Michael Jones

THE APATHY AND THE EMPATHY

They are always very cuddly, and they're always very cute
But to buy the kids a pet is not a trivial pursuit
Just like every living creature, they need love, they need protection
And too many bought on whim become sad victims of rejection
They end their days, uncared for strays, their lives a wretched welter
Their only hope of rescue a benign animal shelter

When first acquired they are desired, the family all love 'Rover'
But when the novelty wears off, then apathy takes over
The children find they've changed their minds, they turn their thoughts to
                                                                    other things
While thoughtless adults just ignore the pain their cold indifference brings
They try to justify their callousness with lame excuses
Subjecting still, that animal to even more abuses

The acquisition of a pet demands consideration
Gives rise to food and exercise, vet's bills and vaccination
A loved and cared for animal will always pay you back in kind
To stroke their fur, evoke their purr, can help to soothe a troubled mind
Cat, dog, or what? It matters not the pets with which your life is shared
Take them into both home and heart, don't start your venture unprepared

This world, for some, may well become a place that's sad and lonely
With family gone they struggle on, themselves to care for only
A cold and empty cheerlessness pervades their every waking hour
But loyal companionship of pets can generate a magic power
So be aware that care breeds care, that love will loneliness relieve
Then joint respect bonds man and pet, and guarantees that neither grieve.

Ron Beaumont

MY BEST FRIEND BOB

He came wrapped in a blanket fine
Small of face with a little whine
I cuddled him within my grasp
And to my bosom I did clasp
I hadn't got a name for him
Bill of Bob or just plain Jim
He poked his nose out of his rug
And at my ear did start to tug
He licked my face and hands with glee
At last he really belongs to me
I'll take him walks and brush his hair
Look after him with loving care
When we both grow up together
We'll still go out whatever the weather
I'll pat his head when he is good
Not hurt him when I am in a mood
I'll teach him well how to obey
To sit and stand and when to stay
I've decided I will call him Bob
Short to handle, just the job
If I treat him tenderly
He'll always be a friend to me.

Marion Pollitt

DEATH OF AN INNOCENT

Hen pheasant struts through the grass,
Broods all raised summer's nearly past
Five sons, seven daughters, she's raised
Now they're gone their separate ways
Alone she feeds in a stubble field
Accepting eagerly, what the good earth will yield
From a secret hide comes a deafening bang
Hen pheasant falls to the gun of man.

Brian Rysdale

THE ZOO ONCE ONLY

I looked at him.
He looked at me,
cold eyes distraught,
demented with longing,
and primeval knowledge of another age,
futilely dangling by one listless arm
from a barren branch inside his cage.
Lack-lustre brown fur, unkempt with mange!
Would that he could be free to range
swinging madly through the greenwood glades,
round and round the sycamore tree,
round and round the sycamore tree.
I looked at him:
he looked at me.
I shall never forget how he looked at me.

Ruby Midwinter

THE FROZEN POND

The village pond was frozen as people hurried by
Its surface was a sheet of ice, mirroring the sky.
Then came the sound of flapping wings through the icy air
As three ungainly ducks appeared and landed unaware.

With feet outstretched before them, feathered wings outstanding,
They slid across the solid ice in a perfect pancake landing.

Feathers ruffled, tails a-twitch, they struggled to their feet,
But on that slippery surface it was no mean feat.
Children's laughter on the air echoed with clarity
As the ducks quacked in annoyance at their gross indignity.

Pauline J Anderson

WHAT'S A PANDA DADDY

What's a panda Daddy?
well a long time ago, they used to roam through china
they're all gone now, and why, I just don't know
I think that I read some where, pollution killed them off
but that was oh, so long ago, before I got this cough.

Are whales still swimming in the sea?
I think so but it's not clear, as poisons from the factories
made many disappear
How can poisons from the factories, hurt fishes in the sea?
well it's very complicated, and no one's quite explained to me

Well can you tell me daddy, are rain forests still around
At school our teacher wasn't sure but in this book I found
It say's a long time ago, there were forests large and green
Filled with exotic birds and animals, and plant we never seen
Where did they all go daddy? Is it true I'll never see
Real live moving animals, like we see on TV

I saw a movie once, that spoke of acid rain
and it killed off nearly all the trees that never grew again
and the men dug up the forests, for the cities you see there
It seems the worlds too small for us, and animals to share.

Couldn't you stop them daddy? Didn't you even try
Did no one help the Wildlife? Is the Bible just a lie
God made the world for all of us, for man and beast to roam
Surely he would never mean for us to make their home
there was nothing much that I could do that's why politicians talk
come on baby, put your face mask on, and lets go for a walk.

Don Woods

BESS

A faithful, friendly pet, oh yes
That was our beautiful springer named Bess
We took her in when no one cared
Our home, our love, with her we shared
The chewed up shoes, the cushions torn
Why didn't she pick on something worn?
Angry as she made me feel
A look is all it took to heal
These things can all be bought anew
But dogs like Bess, there are so few
The years go by, she grows so old
Slowing down, not now so bold
Then came that awful, fateful day
When to the vet's we made our way
No cure for Bess was there to be
We say goodbye, she's now pain free
The tears they stop, the pain does go
For I was very lucky to know

A beautiful springer named Bess

S M Sutton

A NEED FOR LOVE

Born a dog was it a sin,
I was beaten and kicked then dumped in a bin,
I feed from the scraps left at your feet,
I search for warmth and run alone in the street,
Till the comfort my new family brings,
A dish a rug and plenty of playthings,
Why doesn't everyone want us to have,
The loyalty we can give all we need is your love.

Jacqueline Scripps

THE ELEPHANT

Why do we abuse the elephant? Such a noble creature
In so many walks of life we see the elephant feature
Labouring in far eastern countries pulling fallen trees
In India transporting Maharajah's, a colourful sight to please
Seen in circus and zoo giving children much pleasure
The noble elephant we should all treasure.

The nearest in appearance to Prehistoric creatures they may be
And to see their slaughter for ivory is a very sad sight to see
What right has man got to carry out such a deed
In order to satisfy his commercial greed
Surely we have no need to be seen wearing ivory adornment
Or display in our homes ivory ornament

Let these magnificent leviathans roam the plains free
As nature intended we should all clearly see
After all the elephant will not hunt man
Therefore we should see to it that they are unmolested if we can

Den Biggs

A RED SQUIRREL

On an October morning, cut
From some stained glass window, I walked
By the blue clash of the river,
Heard above me in the trees a sudden rustling.
I looked up to catch a bristling rusted brush
Paddling along a fragment of twig. The squirrel saw me
Froze, two sloeberry eyes shining with questions,
Then chattered away in angry Arabic,
Leapt from a precipice of pine
Out into the middle of nowhere, and crashed,
Safe in a roof of leaves. A wink later, gone,
Vanished, the forest's eye closed tight behind.

Kenneth C Steven

THE POUND

Walking down the road all alone
I'm looking for a new and better home.
I was never fussed or never fed
They used to beat me around the head
I'm still looking for this home of mine
With a little help I will be doing fine
I am sitting waiting in the pound
My mum and dad have not been found
Because they have journeyed far away
And have left me on my own to stray
So here I am on my own
Looking for someone to take me home
People come and people go
So far they have all said no.
There was one couple the other day
Who have decided to take me home to stay
For hours I have travelled in this car
And have journeyed very far
I see my house and it looks so grand
She grabs my lead and her husband's hand
Here I have so much to do
Evening I settle and nibble his shoe
Most nights I lay on my new owner's bed
And to be quite honest I'm overfed
So now I'm never left alone
I'm in my new and better home.
                                    Woof!

Victoria McMurray

THE SEAL

I've whiskers and a sleek fur coat,
Plus bags of sex appeal.
My big sad eyes cause hearts to melt
For most folk love a seal.
I'm very fond of ball games,
For balance I'm renowned,
Yet though I am a mammal
I'm clumsy on the ground.
But watch me in the water,
My grace is bound to thrill,
I'm poetry of motion,
A fisherman of skill.
As fish in panic scatter
Much turbulence I cause,
And picking off my victims
I hunt them without pause.
I twist, and dive, and surface,
Then twist and dive again.
No fish can thus outsmart me
For I've a mammal's brain,
And when my meal is over
I feel content inside.
It's then I clean my whiskers
And preen myself with pride,
As watching sparkling patterns
Produced by sea and sun,
I bask upon a rock and think
A seal's life's rather fun.

Richard J Bradshaw

THE BUTTERFLY

Butterfly on winged flight,
Capturing spangled shafts of light.
Hither and thither, struggling to be free,
Rising high on thermal flow -
Descending low for all to see -
Alighting momentarily its shuddering stay,
So fragile brief - no hand can calm.

Patricia Thompson

OUR LITTLE HOUDINI

Alice our first hamster arrived in a box already well chewed!
Her efforts to escape us like a tenacious Houdini she pursued,
For such a little being she needed an armour plated cage and padlocks,
Her appetite for personal bedding ranged from bedroom curtains to socks!
Her day of freedom came at last! Through old pipe holes in the floor,
Relentlessly we kept a vigil sure we'd see Alice no more,
The kindly man from the RSPCA advised us by telephone,
'Drop some bacon rind tied to string down the hole,
That should entice your hamster to come home!'
Recorder music was piped down the hole, a flashlight to guide her shone,
We pulled up the string from the hole, sure enough the bacon had gone!
Two days later up popped Alice, her little nose black, hands all grimey,
We enticed her into her cage with sunflower seeds,
Snap! Went the cage doors, dad laughed 'Rat catchers, blimey!'
She packed her cheeks fit to burst, she slept for hours on end,
We reinforced her cage with wire, the sort she couldn't bend,
We carefully watched her, so did the cat! For two more fleeting years,
She died on a Good Friday, we had a funeral and all shed many tears,
For Alice our little Houdini we placed a satin ribbon on her grave,
Thanked her for the love she made us feel and such happy
Memories we can save.

Joyce M Hefti-Whitney

CAESAR

I see my dog upon the floor
A beautiful golden Labrador,
His legs that once were firm and straight
In age take on an awkward gait,
I think of days when he was young
And jumping for wasps his nose was stung,
His boundless energy chasing a ball
And he wouldn't come when I did call,
When the time has come for him to go
That I will miss him well I know,
But I'll try very hard not to be sad
I'll remember him young, for that I'll be glad.

Audrey K Price

A SEAL'S PERIL

Flippery tails, skim the seas,
Beautiful big, round eyes.
A silvery fish leaps out of the water,
The clear blue skies.

Groups of seals,
Roll in the heat,
Enjoying the midday sun
Baby seals play in the sea,
Having such fun.

A sinister ship passes by,
Leaving a long trail of oil,
The seals are covered from head to tail,
How they toil,
This cannot go on anymore,
Can't humankind see what they spoil?

Sarah Clarke (14)

BOB'S DENTAL CARE

Five-year-old Jack has no concept of germs
He's been known to lick fingers, after playing with worms
And though he's told often, to take much more care
His habits continue, and he's quite unaware

He came down one morning, from brushing his teeth
Wiping Bob's mouth with a clean handkerchief
(Bob is our twelve-year-old golden retriever
Who has just recovered from glandular fever)

'I've brushed my teeth' said Jack, with a grin
'And while I was there, I did Bob's for him'
As you'd imagine, I was quite horrified
The risk of infection, could not be denied!

I threw out Jack's toothbrush, as soon as I knew
And bought him a new one, in a cool shade of blue
A week or so later, when going to bed
Jack leaned over, kissed me, and said:

'Why did I need a new toothbrush, mum?'
'Because,' I replied, 'you might just succumb
to a deadly disease, passed on by your pet
Heaven only knows, just what you could get!'

Then Jack said, 'But I wouldn't catch germs from old Bob
I'd never use *my* toothbrush, for doing the job!
I remembered all of those things that you'd said
So I made up my mind to use your brush instead!'

Margaret Sanderson

REBEL RABBIT

We found him in a car park, about three years ago
Although we advertised the fact, no one seemed to want to know
The big white Bunny Rabbit was looking rather lost
So we took him home with us, not knowing then, the cost
Three bunnies we already had but one had lost his mate
So this one went in 'Choco's' hutch, down by the garden gate

We watched them get aquatinted and everything seemed fine
Especially for 'Choco' for now he wouldn't pine
The other two were wary and they had a right to be
They could sense he'd made his mind up, to be The Boss you see
They're let out on the lawn each day so they can run around
And were quite content to nibble grass, except the one we'd found

The garden had a fence round to protect expensive flowers
But 'Rebel' was a digger, so they disappeared in hours
Rose trees were uprooted 'cause they were in his way
He could have dug the Channel Tunnel in a single day
Devastation everywhere, then he jumped the garden wall
To start excavating next door's garden, they weren't pleased at all

Now we can't leave the back door open on a sunny day
He devastates inside the house in the same destructive way
The stereo deck stopped working, and then we found out why
He'd bitten thru' electric wires, could have blown the house sky high
His face was speckled with black spots, and now his fur's turned grey
We fixed a small gate by the door, but he's dragged that away

Then he went missing for a day, thought we'd see him no more
Till someone knocked to tell us he was waiting at front door
Have you ever had the feeling 'Oh Lor! Not him again'
You know there'll be more trouble but you don't know where or when
So . . . we call him 'Rebel Rabbit' and if he don't like that name
He can hop off! Down the car park, the place from whence he came.

Bell Ferris

YESTERDAY'S HERO

Look into my eyes Master, what do you see?
A faded old dog, just looking at thee.
Coat much less shining, face spattered with grey,
A body less shapely, tail not so gay.
Look into my eyes Mistress, what do you see?
What are you thinking when you're looking at me?
I remember my young days, Mum, sister and me,
Just being naughty with brothers all three.
Don't you remember, or have you forgot
All the fun and the games, how we laughed such a lot.
Those times at the weekends when show days begun,
You called me 'Your Champion' when those red cards we won.
I gave you my babies, but now they're all grown,
Their young are now rearing young ones of their own.

Look into my face Master, what do you see?
A little old dog still looking at thee.
No time now for walkies, no time for a chat,
Just my dinner and bed, and sometimes a pat.
These days are for young ones, you show it you see,
You never spend time now, not even with me.
I'm old and uncertain, and not very wise,
And gaze at the door with far away eyes.
You spoke then I'm certain, your lips made a word,
But like my eyes that are failing, my ears never heard.
The days are so short now, the days go so fast,
Remember dear people that nothing can last.
So open your eyes people, open and see,
Not a faded old dog, see me, just me
I will love you forever,
Will you always love me?

Tina Homes

OUR PIGEON, OUR PLEASURE

It was *our* pleasure to have lived with a bird
A pigeon she was, this sounds absurd,
But she was injured, we found her in pain
The vet set her wing but all was in vain
'It must come off it is injured so badly'
As the vet spoke we looked on so sadly,
'She depends on you it is your decision
You must keep her warm and make provision'
What could we do?
We knew right away the onus was ours
When we found her that day.

She adapted well with one wing less,
She lived in the house with not much mess,
A cage in the lounge was her bed at night
Close to the cat they got on alright
She loved us she came to our call
Seven years with us she spent in all,
She played in the garden when we gave her a bath
And fluttered her wing to make us laugh.
If a visitor came she would give them a fright
As her party piece was to give a good bite

This bird we found taught us many a thing
As she struggled to fly with only one wing
Determined she was with great strength of will
As the poor little soul overcame such an ill.
But she lived her life in her own unique way
We attended her needs each single day.
Her life was spent with care and love
Now she flies in Heaven above.

Carol Shaikh

MY LITTLE FRIEND THE SPIDER

My little friend the spider
Has lived inside my van,
He moves around and spins his web
The neatest that he can.
With to and from he moves around
As I flit from place to place,
With round, and round, and up and down
He meets me face to face.
I wouldn't like to hurt him
As you can plainly see,
It's not all pets that stay around,
But I guess that he likes me.

Jeannette McShane

HONEY

I've got a pal her name is Honey
I love her very much
When she snuggles up to me
I love her gentle touch

Honey is a nice old thing
It's surprising the love that she can bring
As I take her out for my morning ride
I sit on the saddle with my heart filled with pride

As I go riding up the lane
People turn round and call out her name
Honey is known by all around
Even as far as the nearest town

I take her home to have her rest
So in the morning she can look her best
Then I give her a good brushing down
And I give her a kiss and go into town

Bert Booley

DE-FLEAING THE CAT

Flea season is upon us again,
It's time to de-flea the cat.
But how to do it successfully,
Without being scratched.

I put the fleas on the pill,
Carefully mixed it into the dish.
Cat took a sniff and gave me *that look*,
'Are you trying to poison me?' it hissed.

I grabbed a pot of powder,
A job to be done outside.
I breathed in the dust and started to cough,
And the cat ran away to hide.

I held the front legs, he held the back,
While one of us aimed with the spray.
Cat hated the noise and started to struggle,
And caused a whopping affray.

I grabbed a tissue and very gently,
The blood from our wounds wiped.
And wondered why, no-one's invented,
Flea-gone impregnated wet wipes.

With coast all clear, cat sneaks back in,
And settles down on the mat.
Would it notice what's wrapped round the hand,
As it's stroked and given a pat.

Helusia Shire

TO SUSIE
(A Wood Green Rescue)

At the shelter, there she sat
Just a little tabby cat
Nothing more (or less) than that!

On the very day we met,
I had gone to choose a pet;
Never sure what I would get.

I was standing near the door,
When she lifted one small paw,
The, two lovely eyes I saw.

Such a loving cat is she
It is very pain to see,
How she captivated me!

Though she brings me eschewed mice,
Which is never really nice,
I forgive her this one vice.

She emits a gentle 'purr-rr,'
When I make a fuss of her
As I softly stroke the fur.

Without doubt, it's fair to say
Life has changed in every way,
Since my Susie came to stay.

Phyllis Kirk

DOG

My paws are wet, and I feel so cold,
no one loves me, because I'm tired and old.
They just got fed up, they left me in the road,
they lost all the love, at first they had showed.
Now I'm in kennels, waiting my fate,
hope someone comes, before it's too late.
You see I've got one day, then I will die,
I hope it won't hurt, if it does I will cry.
But wait, a little girl's seen me, she's giving me a treat,
by the look on her face, she thinks that I'm sweet.
And her family, all looking at me,
They're taking me home,
I'm going to be free.

Rachel Oxtoby

WINNIE

We love our old dog Winnie, she is faithful
through and through, the things she does is quite
unique, she melts our hearts in two.

When Winnie's in the garden she wards off unwelcome
folk, she growls and barks at passers by, no one
with her would cope.

When Winnie's told to sit and stay she obeys without
a thought, those commands she's given are like play to
her, her love cannot be bought.

The friendship shown from our old Win is really
quite unique, the love she gives is also there if
only Win could speak.

Sue Curtis

53

ODE TO A DUCK

She lay dear in the mud, her chicks swimming around
Unaware of their tragic loss.
The drake stood by trying to nudge her up.
It brought a tear to your eye.
Along came a Mum with two little kids
To watch the ducks in the burn.
They'd come with some bread to feed the birds
When they noticed she was dead.
The children cried 'What can we do
The poor little things might die.'
'We must rescue the ducks before they are harmed'
Was the ultimate cry.
So Mother and bairns went into the brook,
Wading right up to the middle,
Caught each little bird in a butterfly net,
Then gave it a hug and a cuddle.
The fluffy ducklings flotilla, ten babies in all,
A sight to stir your heart.
'Take them home in that box, very carefully now
You can put them in the bath.'
The children wept when the people came
To collect the dear little souls.
They'll give them some shelter, some food and some water
Until they can fend for themselves.
We're really so sad she's no longer there,
She gave us so much pleasure
As year after year she hatched her brood
A memory we'll always treasure.

Rhoda Glanville

GOODBYE MY SHEEPDOG

Goodbye my bonnie dog
You've earned the rest my friend.
So sleep, in your eternal sleep
Your strife, is at an end.

The sands of time, will forever run
And the years will come to pass.
But I'll never see your likes again
My bonnie canine lass.

I still see your running across the fields
Bringing sheep to pen.
And the way you always wagged your tail
When work was at an end.

It pained me so much, when you tried to stand
So strong in your endeavour.
For you tried your best in your distress
But your legs had gone for ever.

When I saw the sadness in your eyes
I felt your canine anguish.
I knew your bark, was a cry for help
For I understood your language.

Goodbye my bonnie lass
See, you have your master crying.
But, tears on face, is no disgrace.
When you love the dog that's dying.

Matt McGinn

ROSIE

Words dried up
Those that stay, encapsulated in gloom
I should have known it would be like this
The third time around
The feeling of despair
I didn't play *God*
But bowing to the knowledge of the professionals
That her saucy look
The placing of her feet when defying me
The wobble of her lovely bum when she walked off in a huff
The shiny cap of her head smooth and gleaming would be no more
No more devotion
No more those eyes following me everywhere
A constant companion to me and the stove
Me, food, and warmth, her world
Now to be no more
A dark afternoon spuming with rain
I knew what love was in that clinical room
Knew as I stayed with her till her pain eased
My mouth against that smooth sweet smelling head
She knew I was with her
She knew I loved her
Dried up words must be written and I will grieve
But now
I must take up the weapons against life again
And show on this new year a glacial face
But I will always remember my *Rosie*
Always remember what it was like the third time
Knowing each time it gets worse
St Francis love her as I did . . .

Joan Eyles

ODE TO MY CATS

Sleek and slender, with eyes of green
trying your hardest not to be seen,
under the bushes you hide and watch
waiting for a stray leaf to catch and play.

Tigger and George my best friends are they
understanding every word I say,
fur so soft and whiskers so sleek
one is wild and one is meek.

They wait and watch for me to come home
with a cat you are never alone,
they cheer me up when I am down
always knowing when to be around.

Tigger's my nurse when I am ill
curled up beside me till I am well.

Loyalty and love my cats give me
if only people could give love so free,
George black and white, proud and cool,
he always shows he's nobody's fool.

Tigger's my tabby fierce and wild,
but with me he's a baby, just like my child
I love my cats as they love me,
and without a cat I can never be.

May Strike

JUST FOR JUDY

When I got told the news today
That Judy my dog had died
Part of my childhood disappeared
And my heart was broken inside
Judy my dog, my little friend
We had so many happy years
You were always there to cheer me up
But now you can't stop my tears
Even though you've gone away
Your memories remain with me still
The memories are locked deep in my heart
I love you and always will

Patricia Pratt

TO GEMMA - AN ORDINARY TABBY

So many years of faithfulness you gave to us my friend
Your love undimmed though old and aged you were towards the end,
And memory glides across the years to when you came our way.
Injured and abandoned, a lost unhappy stray.
But soon you took us to your heart and made our hearts your own
And ever after through the years affection knew no bounds.
Your young and vital life with ours along life's way was merged.
We loved the joy you gave to us - so many memories surge
As I look back across the years we shared in constant trust
I thank you warm and loving friend for all you gave to us.
And now no more your bright eyes shine a greeting all your own.
A silent mound beneath the trees, a silent slab of stone.
Our dear Lord gave no hint or word that Heaven you would share,
But surely in His mercy I shall wake to find you there.

Patricia Ruffle

OUR CAT

It was a cold and dirty morning
When we saw the face that day
Peering in the back door
And wouldn't go away.

The face was so appealing
Although it looked quite thin
We did what most of us would do
Opened up and let it in.

This went on day by day
It soon became a habit
When we started feeding it
With tins of beef and rabbit.

By now we were acquainted
She seemed to like us too
So with a short discussion
We knew what we would do.

We traced her rightful owner
Not to cause a fuss
Who said if she was happy
It's best she stayed with us.

So now there are the three of us
We talk to her all day
And though it sounds ridiculous
She seems to know just what we say.

So we hope she stays as happy
As I'm sure we'll like her more
Than the first day that we saw her face
Pressed closely to the door!

H H Smith

CHOOSING A FRIEND

Off we went to our local pound
Where all unwanted dogs are found
There they are in little cages
All types colours breeds and ages
Husband whispers remember just one
Before my choosing had begun
When I looked what did I see
So many faces watching me
Ears flopped down all looking sad
All awaiting to be had
Whining and howling as we pass by
I felt myself begin to cry
Suddenly I see this tiny face
So lonely staring into space
We both look and walk away
Hearing a whine and bark that seemed to say
Please will you take me away
Going back what do we see
One that's longing to be free
That's the one I tell my spouse
So now that pet lives in our house
She's settled in and here to stay
We're so happy we chose her on that day

Merril Morgan

THE PURR

I heard a noise behind my chair,
At first it gave me quite a scare.
It sounded like a motorbike,
Whose engine needed tuning, like.

I turned around and saw my cat
Asleep upon his favourite mat.
How one so small makes such a row
I just can't explain anyhow.

He purrs sometimes while he's asleep
Or when upon the bed he'll creep
To prod my face with his soft paw
To ask me for some food once more.

With this glad sound he welcomes me
And comes to sit upon my knee.
It is a noise I love to hear,
For then I know my cat is near.

Catherine Gleadow

WINTER SADNESS

The field stands white
with frost, and the bitter
wind has become my companion.
On the horizon, I watch a fox
whose injuries have reduced her
near to death.

Slowly she crawls close to the
ground, rubbing her blood stained
belly upon the earth. But the frost
does not want to hold or nurse her,
and still she lies her soul now
gliding toward the afterlife.
Droplets of crimson blood seeps
like a stream gently from the fresh
carcass, whilst the savage wind softly
kisses its breath across the vixen's thick
fur.

Winter has arrived and so to has darkness,
which comes in the shape of man's savage lust
for wildlife destruction. And for myself now
stood over the fox's body, I shed sombre tears
of spirit sorrow.

Jeffrey Woods

TAMARA

You sat there behind bars in the pouring rain,
Eyes flashing yellow, I'll never be tame,
The only one there that came to the front, we knew then that you were
the one,
A donation and a signature is all it took, we had to go out and buy a book.

You travelled in a cardboard box, a paw sticking out of a hole,
meowing piteously all the way home,
You sat on the landing not daring to move, oh my we had a lot to prove,
Whiskers and cuddles finally bought you down, you started exploring, and
made all around your own.

Then one day in January you bumped into the wall - off to the vet we travelled,
whatever you did do to deserve this we have never been able to unravel..
Tests and prodding you took it all, that's when we confirmed that you were
special my little puddy, better than them all.

Even now blind you gave us so much, following and waiting for affection
Even when we moved furniture you found your armchair with perfection.
The window sill was also your spot, hearing the car off you would trot,
waiting for the key to rattle in the door, you would be off into the garden once
more.

Your craving for adventure never ceased, in fact your need to escape under the
gate seemed to increase,
Your eyes still flashing you prowled your territory, seeing off intruders with
such energy.

Well my darling it's time to say goodbye, with a final cuddle,
We'll never forget the star called Tamara, Tam, Tammy, Puddy, Chuffy, Pud la
cat and all those other names mentioned in love,
The hardest decision it was to make, but I know the right one for your sake.

We just hope from there up above, you enjoyed living with us as much as we enjoyed having you.
You'll never be forgotten.

Goodbye darling, see you tomorrow.

Kim Still

STRAY DOG OR STRAY CAT

Another lost, lonely soul
Wandering the streets on unfamiliar pavements,
Getting hollered at and kicked about by uncaring humans;
Tormented cruelly by children on the way.
So sad!
So sad!
Rummaging about dustbin bags for food,
And drinking from muddy puddles.
Wandering on and getting further away from home . . .
And sighing hopelessly inside:
'Where's my Mammy?' or
'Where's my Daddy?'
And them, Mammy and Daddy, desperately asking all:
'Have you seen my precious cat?' or
'Have you seen my darling dog?'
And looking on with tearful eyes and heavy heart at the shaking heads:
Ever,
Ever,
Shaking heads;
But, continuing the search.
Never ever giving up the search.
Asking on, and constantly praying and hoping inside for good news, and
A miracle to happen

Amen.

Mary Pauline Winter

A RESCUE DOG'S STORY

A loving home was given to me,
Abundance of walks and regular tea,
Lots of fuss and lots of care
Lots of titbits for me to share.

But now the attention seems to fail,
No response to my wagging tail,
An open door, and a command to go!
What have I done? I do not know.

I scratch the door and bark and cry
But no-one answers, why oh why?
I wander around frightened and lonely,
Looking for someone to love and to hold me.

Alone in the rain, cold and the sleet,
Sore hungry belly and sores on my feet.
I lie in the puddles and curl up real tight
Praying the angels will take me tonight.

Why did they say they loved me, and *lie*,
Why have they left me alone here to *die?*
Someone has touched me, a hand I don't know
Into the care of *Petsearch* I go.

A welcoming hug, and a warm cosy bed,
A doggy doctor, and I'm lovingly fed,
I'm happy again, and chasing my ball,
A new loving home - thank you to *you all.*

Paula M Atherton

THE DOG THAT WANTED A YELLOW TAG

Here comes another stray dog
It goes into the pen
A bit nervous at first
Then it sees another dog
And runs off at a burst
The other dog barks as if to say 'Hello'
It says 'I've been here a long time
But you might be lucky and go
We see a lot of faces
And some are very nice
If only they would take me
I'd be their sugar and spice
My owners didn't want me
Which made me very sad
I only chewed their slippers
Which made them very mad
I hope today someone will come along and say
Put a yellow tag on
I want to take this one away.'

Suzanne Cooke (10)

NON-PEDIGREE TABBY

Your beauty is outstanding
Your markings quite exquisite
You're noisy and demanding
But gentle and loving with it.

I wouldn't swap your style and grace
For all the tea in China
No pedigree could take your place
For there is no cat finer.

Sarah Jane Lane

WILL RAIN

We saw a horse in a field
It was all skin and bone
I'd wanted a horse for so long
One I could call my own

My dad went to see the owner
The deal was all cut and dried
But it would take a lot of work
To get him fit to ride.

We found out it was a racehorse
His name was Will Rain
How could they let him get like this
So skinny and lame.

Now he's improved so much
He's getting harder to control
He gets so very excited
He has far too much go.

In the end we all decide
A race is what he's needing
On the day I cannot watch
But they tell me that he's leading.

The finish line approaches
The others are gaining fast
But he keeps his head in front
As the finish line they pass.

Lisa Suzanne

THE TERRIER'S TALE

The woman thought she'd breed from me
To bring in lots of money.
But living in that pit of hell
Was anything but funny.

I never did become a stud
It wasn't meant to be
The fashions changed, pit bulls the rage
She had no use of me.

Out on the streets throughout the day
I roamed amongst the dregs
One night she hurled me down the stairs
I've pins in both my legs.

A rescue centre saw my plight
And spared me from that fate.
Another home was found for me
And life became just great.

A comfy bean bag for my nest
A sleeping bag on top.
I'm walked, I'm fed, tucked up in bed
I'm just an old milk sop.

Such love has quite transformed my life
The bad old days are over.
I chase the bunnies, go on hols,
In fact I live in clover.

Christine Turner

FIREWORKS NIGHT

I'm sitting here all alone with only my dog
Outside it is cold, the streets all filled with fog
The fireworks are making, such a loud noise
You can hear the cheers of the girls and boys.
They're all enjoying themselves, while I'm feeling sad
My dog is not well, she's looking so bad.
She used to be lively, so brave and so bold
But now she looks fragile, so gentle and old.
A lump on her leg the vets can do nothing,
Everything she does she just ends up puffing.
Then she falls over and her leg it is cut
There is blood all over, so I bandage her up
I'm crying so hard, I can't hardly see
But she still licks, as if she's comforting me
My mum comes home and puts her in the car
'It's okay' she said 'the vet's is not far.'
I wait for mum to bring her home
But when she arrives she's all alone
Her eyes red and full of tears
We've had old Lass for 16 years.
We mourned our dog for so long, our lives felt so empty
But now we have good memories, of those there are plenty.

Joanne Marie McManamon

THE TORTOISE

Can you see her in the dell?
Oak and amber is her shell,
There the tortoise lies asleep
'Neath roots and leaves through winter deep.

She wakes in spring
Seeks sun-warmed stones,
Then lies on them to heat her bones.

Her scaley head comes out and in
Her neck is soft with leathery skin.
Wisdom shines from black bead eyes
A hundred years until she dies.

Holly Turnbull (9)

FROM AFRICA TO WOOD GREEN

W andering across the African plains
O kapi, zebra and gazelle
O utmanoeuvre lions that freely roam
D evoid of cage - kings at home

G orillas that stand so silent and strong
R un openly through forests - but for how long?
E lephants slayed for their ivory tusks, we are
E ach responsible
N ature gives only so much

A cross the continents animals roam free but
N ot all are so lucky so please come and see
I n cages they wait for a new start
M any abandoned - so please have a heart
A nd come take a look and see if you find
L ove for an animal of any kind

S uch is the work of the Animal Shelter
H elping to make life so much better for
E ach of the animals placed in their care who are
L ooking for love - it's all that they ask although
T he finding of homes is quite a task but
E veryone can be a helper by
R emembering the Wood Green Animal Shelter

Patricia O'Gorman

JACK NECKED

We share our bed with Jack, a ménagerie à trois
He makes up in affection what he lacks in looks
Physique was not improved by heavy lorries
His head, nearly symmetrical, has one unbroken tooth
One good eye, but the white of the other rolls loose

Our daily ritual
Down to breakfast when he wraps around my neck
Legs dangling like a lion, extraordinary face pressed close to mine
One eye, loving, but unnerving, stares
And the cracked purr deafens as we totter down the stairs

That day, not ready to descend
For cat-neck toilet is not easy
I distance Jack, poised on chest of drawers
Careless concentration carries me too close
And Jack springs, a flying neck holder

Broken claws
Efficient brakes in a soft shoulder

Nicholas Hutton

LEARN FROM THE ANIMALS

Fight to protect their mate and their home,
care for their young
till old enough to roam,
clean their nest their den their dray,
socialise with their kind the rest of the day.
Fight through drink, through drugs through lust
we must have more, we must, we must,
greed and envy, power and hate
this we must stop before it's too late,
learn from the animals this we must do,
It's the only way forward for me and for you.

Keith Slatter

GEORGE

I watch my small cat sleeping,
Touch him gently, and he purrs;
Black and white paw across one eye,
Curled round snug as he prefers.

I think of springtime blossoms
On the apple tree, and how
A face peeps round the nest box,
George lies waiting on the bough.

I can feel the summer sunshine
Reflecting ripples on the pond,
George leaps upwards as a dragonfly
Skims over and beyond.

I can see the autumn colours,
Dead leaves carpeting the ground;
George hears a rustle by the hedge
And dives towards the sound.

I remember winter crispness,
George's pawprints cross the snow
They reach the table for the birds
No further do they go!

I watch my small cat sleeping,
Touch him gently, and he purrs;
Half dreaming of his day outdoors
He knows it's me, and hardly stirs.

Karen Swan

RICH CAT

Lucy was a rich cat,
Born on a grand estate,
With every care and comfort,
And plenty of food on her plate.

As a kitten, she was adopted
By a loving professional pair,
Who took her to their mansion,
And she willingly settled there.

Soon she became the top cat;
Kept other cats away.
There was only one big problem,
The couple were out all day.

She visited all the neighbours.
Only one of them seemed alright,
So she spent all her days in their house,
Going back to her home at night.

The elderly neighbours' cat soon died,
So Lucy took over instead.
She has now secured a second home,
And will never be short of a bed.

Ben Hutton

NIGHT-LIFE

Cat against the skyline
Walking across the tiles,
Black and silhouetted
Up among the stars.

Darkness is so friendly
When your eyes shine in the night,
Even though there's danger
Lurking out of sight.

A mouse, a bird, a rabbit
Out there in their park,
Playing, hunting, fighting;
A life in the dark.

Survival of the hunted
Is victory for the dawn,
Another day tomorrow,
Welcome to the morn.

Joan Margaret Howard

HERE IN MY DREAMS

A furry brown shadow
Sits close by me,
Soft paw in my hand,
Black nose on my knee.

Our hearts beat as one
A long time ago.
Oh! Life was such fun
Did she have to go?

Death, the dog-thief
Stole her sadly away,
Shattering my belief
That she'd always stay.

Yet she's here by me now
In my dreams night and day,
And here, I do vow,
She'll always stay

     . . . my faithful brown shadow.

Doneth Benson

EPITAPH FOR EMMA

She was only a dog - black and tan, cold nose, lovely eyes.
A Doberman - Doberbitch I suppose I should say -
In this politically correct world.
And she lay on her side in the grass in the morning,
Legs out as she did in the hearth.
Surely asleep.

She was only a dog - but she didn't come in
And we searched in the night and we called and we looked
But she lay in the grass - surely asleep -
Where we found her in the morning.
And we cried, of course we cried, and we miss her - all of us

She was only a dog - but a loving, trusting, faithful,
Noisy and happy companion - shy and demanding by turns.
Her character imprinted on our family - part of our way of life.
Nothing sentimental - emotional, sure - it happened this morning.
We'll get another, of course we will -
But we miss her sorely.

Godfrey J Curtis

MY CAT

They sneer and say 'It was just a cat
You silly girl, what 'you crying at'
How can they understand what your short life meant to me
Your enchanting little ways - your enduring company
How in the summer sun we would play upon the grass
How in my saddest times only you could make me laugh

By the fire in winter, on the rug you'd snugly purr
Feeling how I loved you as I gently stroked your fur
And spoke to you in pictures of a world so cold and bare
But made so warm and beautiful just by knowing you were there

And now you are with God and I am alone
It was only your presence that made this house my home
I sit still and quiet as the autumn wind grows fierce
Whipping up the dank, dead leaves with its whistling howls and shrieks

Staring out of the window, I think I see you by the tree
I look again, but all is bare, accept for dancing leaves
So now we're apart my true and tiny friend
But I know some day our souls, will surely meet again

Yvonne Notholt

SERENITY OF DOLPHINS

As I close my eyes I can always imagine
The freedom of dolphins living in the ocean
I admire their style beauty and grace
As they swim along at a steady pace

I love to see them rise up from the ocean
Stretching upwards to meet with the heavens
Their backs are arched full of grace and beauty
Dancing in mid air like it was their duty

They descend back down to meet with the ocean
And the water explodes with an upwards motion
Waving their tails out as if they are dancing
Twisting and turning just like their romancing

Bonding loved ones together side by side
Mother and father with baby they glide
United they swim through the shimmering sea
Looking so happy and completely free

Then I watched them for a repeat performance
As they rise up from the deep blue ocean
Repeating themselves day after day
Showing us humans how love can be.

Gillian Stannard

FURRY FOUR PAWS TIMES TWO

Tiny black kitten, large pink mouth,
Opens wide - no sound comes out.
A look, a glance, is all it takes
For the broken heart to race.

Look away before she purrs.
(Oh, delight of coal-black furs!)
Look again and love may start,
To help to mend your broken heart.

Her whiskers twitch and from within
A mighty purr you hear begin
Pick her up - she nestles close,
I guess this kitten is just 'the most'!

Home she comes
            It's not same.
Back to Wood Green
            We go again.

Small black kitten, tiny toes
Bright pink pads and button nose,
Yellow amber eyes that shine
Looking deeply into mine.

Hold her close
            She purrs away
Our second cat
            Comes home to stay.

M Riches

TO 'CLOVA' - A SPRINGER SPANIEL

You are thirteen and a half
And not a grey hair!
We said we would grow old together - remember?
Seven years of your life to one of mine.
But I'm now lined and long-since grey
While you have kept your puppy face;
Long silken ears and big brown eyes
Still make you irresistible,
As well you know!

'In human years you are ninety four,'
I remind you
As you rummage in your toy-box,
But with triumphant bark, you seize a ring
And toss it in the air
Begging me to play . . .

Beloved companion of heath and hill,
I climb more slowly with the passing years
While you, at first scent of rabbit, are away!
Tirelessly running for miles and miles
Heedless of age and life's brief span.
But always here, if anywhere,
I know your spirit will run free,
And if ever I walk this way alone
You will surely follow me.

Patricia Doreen Graeme

PURRFECTION

God created us felines,
In impeccably purrfect taste,
Designed for lithness and beauty
Charm and silky grace.
With an air of independence
Which we avidly maintain
Causing unconcatable humans
To regard it as distain.
But our purrsons, who admire us,
We cherish and adore
Giving loyalty and friendship
From under our feline paw.
Scientists offer reasons
For our doing this and that,
My knowledge is far greater
'Cause I'm a much loved cat.

Miaow!

Hannah

TIBBY
17th June 1992-8th May 1995

The garden and the house are haunted now:
Your striped shadow slips through the bushes
And your white belly gleams in the dusk
Inviting my hand,
Bereaved of your silken softness and armoured paw.
Your sisters lack your loving playfulness
And my lap your lithe warm weight,
For my big, bold beautiful boy is gone.
The hebe shelters his last long sleep -
And I remember.

G M Wyatt

NEW SONG FOR BROTHER LEO

(Dedicated to Brother Leo Benedict Van Leeuwen, my much loved little spaniel, formerly in the care of Wood Green Animal Shelters and then known as 'Codie', a very brave little dog, who has taught me so much about forgiveness.)

And now little one you must learn how to trust
We will take it so gently I know that we must
You will need lots of time to learn new tender words
I will help you forget all the blows and the hurts
You will always now only hear my gentle voice
You can run now in freedom and wildly rejoice
Forget all your bleak days they are now in the past
From now on little one you'll have love that will last
No more creeping round hungry alone in the dark
You will learn to enjoy life and play in the park
No more nights will be spent in a cold and dark shed
No neglect that half killed you and left you for dead
Because now you are much loved though you've been through hell
And love takes us all of a lifetime to tell
So your days will be spent on the lawn by the flowers
You will dream blissful dreams and snooze gently for hours
You'll be treasured and loved now I promise my dear
And for Love's sake my darling I'll always be here
The last words you'll hear at night will be I love you
You have so much to learn about love that is new
The dark days of your sad past are finished and gone
So please learn now to trust me my loved little one

Joanah Francis

CAT COMFORT

I know a something sweet, and that is
What a *comfortable* thing a cat is!

When nights are long and sleep a-shying
Regard that fuzzy bundle, lying
Nose tucked in tail, relaxed, deep-breathing,
Sublimely sunk and (roundly wreathing)
Soaked in unconsciousness: each padded paw
Unflexed and limp: a muted, gentle snore
The sole indicative of life: his purring
Stilled as he sank in slumber, non-recurring.

I know a something that to me is
Epitome of peace, so tranquil he is!

When wind's a-howl, and rain is stinging
The windowpanes, there lies he singing
Basso profundo in his furry chest,
Spread-eagled by the fire. He knows the best
And softest spot in every room: his form,
Exuding comfort, lives but to be warm.
Full-fed and placid, drowsily replete,
From ear-tip down to tail-tip *cat-complete.*

I know a something wise, and that is -
What a *comfortable thing* a cat is!

Dorothy Fancourt (Decd)

TO 'J R'

You wandered in, a stranger, a fighter, a loner
down on your luck.
We took you to our hearts, took the struggle from
your shoulders for a few brief years but you gave
us more, much more. A trust, an absolute trust you
gave to no one, knowing no one to whom it could be
given. You shared our warm rooms, sought our warm
shoulders, showing in the only way you could, your
trusting love.
And then another struggle loomed, a fight against
your failing body - a puzzle - it never let you
down before. You seemed to win until last night
but you could fight no more and, lying helpless
with beseeching eyes, you purred as if to say,
'Can you help me?' I did, my pet. I gave you
peace in the only way I knew. I gave you death.
If you could only know, dear friend, what you have
given me.

Raymond L Clifford

ALL GOD'S CREATURES

Look deep into our eyes, so the world may see,
That all God's creatures were born to be free.
As free as the birds who fly in the sky,
As free as the wind in God's heavenly sky.
Only to be loved in the way that we should,
And to be respected throughout our lives,
As all God's creatures with a simple life.

H W Fogarty

81

TESTING LABS

Lonely and defenceless
Locked up for life
In a cage

Just for the convenience of humans
Just so they can have their hair dye
And their eye shadow

In an attempt to make themselves look beautiful
They are ruining an animal's life
Killing some poor, helpless creature
Who was unlucky enough
To be brought to the labs

Tormented and humiliated

But what for?
Why are innocent creatures being punished?
What have they ever done
To deserve this torture
And cruelty?

It's got to stop
This moronic treatment to animals

We will fight against it
And prevent this insane behaviour

We will set the animals free
They will learn to live normally
Away from pain and suffering

And any memories of the testing labs
Will just be in nightmares
Of this unbelievable violence
Carried out by humans

Sarah Doberska (14)

TEDDY
(Dedicated to my Teddy)

My friend said get a dog for company
then no more lonely will you be,
To the Animal Shelter we did go
to see what they had to show,
Noisy barking running up and down
some wagged tails others seemed to wear a frown,
Then from a kennel he came so slow
rushed to the wire his eyes aglow,
We looked at each other in that way
his eyes looked into mine as if to say,
Please, please take me from this jail
with head pressed to wire he looked up and wagged his tail,
We fell in love that dog and I
take him? Of course I said with a sigh,
He seemed to know just what was said
his look said thank you, thank you, as home we sped,
We had some lovely days Teddy and me
the love and affection he gave was good to see,
There were times when I did not it return
and my sorrow for that pain in my heart does burn,
Now Ted has gone my life is one that is so sad
but I know he is with another he loved, my dad,
His memory and love will never perish you see
the time will come when again together we will be,
My love to you Ted will again be ever true
and long walks we will take just me and you.

John Clarke

REX

No one could keep the two of us indoors
Rex, my golden dog with freckled paws
When work was done, we would often roam
for hours and hours and many miles from home.

There were the times you really made me cross
Times I wondered in fact who was the boss
then you'd look at me with those golden eyes
full of love, tail wagging, doggy wise.

Oh happy days . . . but soon they had to pass
We couldn't let you suffer at the last
Tearful farewell, and still sad to speak
In another world Rex we shall meet . . .

Valerie Ovais

CONFORMING

Meticulously seeking these fruits to live
Scouring across each blade of grass.
Depicting a scene -
So minute.
Befriending a sparrow,
Wary of the unknown.
Lavishly seeking
Such fruits to fulfil
Her unknown ambition -
To satisfy her hunger
And exist another
Day.
She returns -
And again.

E J Faraday

CATS HAVE FEELINGS TOO

It was my intention to give up cats
But they would not give up on me
Though living in undesirable flats
Still I heard the same recurring plea
About cats who were to be disowned,
Cats they may have to be put down,
Would I please offer them a home,
One by one, the felines came around

I had not wanted cats (or doggies)
Why do I continually collect
A selection of disreputable moggies,
The kind that other folk reject,
It was reported both were angels
With natures gentle and compliant
They were in fact both cross and vengeful
With noses seriously out of joint

They tolerate me, but hate each other,
Now I am the umpire of their brawl
From the moment that they saw each other
It was like gunfight at the OK Corral
Things are not always as they may appear
Who knows what their life has been
Perhaps they are not fierce, just insecure,
I don't take sides, just intervene

Now tempers are mellow, coats well-groomed,
As individuals they have improved
I suppose that it must be assumed
That cats have feelings too
So now we all live here together
And things are fine, lest I forget,
That to stop the fur from flying,
I have to keep the dears apart

Margaret Garvey

FAITHFUL FRIENDS

Little dog with the pleading eyes,
Looking into mine,
Saying 'I've been badly treated,
Won't you please be kind?'

Little dog with the soulful eyes,
You are nought but skin and bone,
You say to me 'Don't leave me,
Please will you take me home?'

'All I want is your love and care,
And a warm basket by the fire,
A run out in the open air,
And a full bowl, is all I desire.'

Little dog with the crying eyes,
I've been hurt like you,
I can understand the suffering,
That you have been through.

I'm happy to provide for you,
All your simple needs,
Food and drink, a cosy bed,
A collar, and a lead.

For I know that you'll repay me,
With more than money can buy,
A faithful and trusting companion,
Always at my feet to lie,

Little dog, I rescued you,
When your life was near an end,
And you saved me from my loneliness,
You are my one true friend.

Brenda Wilding

TIGER

Honey golden velvet
Slinking through the grass,
Shadowed by its blackened stripes
From prey that comes to pass.

Emerald eyes bejewel the face
Edged with pure white fur.
Composure is of the essence
So regal and demure.

Muscles tensed, prepared to spring,
Speed is locked inside.
Beautiful but deadly,
A killer that can glide.

Chris Harris

TO LILA WITH LOVE
(Written to my beloved dog with affection)

Thank you dear friend for your welcome
To me, as I come through the door
Your lovely brown eyes say, 'I love you'
What could I wish for more?

Thank you dear friend for your love
You give to me each passing day
The love of a dog never changes
No matter what people may say.

Thank you dear Lila for your friendship
Your constancy never grows cold
The price of your loyal devotion
Is worth more than silver or gold.

Mary Ferguson

SIXPENCE AND THE GALE

Sad dog I am today
and on my little bed do lie
Looking out on darkened sky
wishing I could 'out to play'.
I've chewed my rug and Momma's shoe
and now I don't know what to do.
The wind is blowing 'neath the door
wish I could stop it with my paw!
Out there the rain is pelting down
enough to make a poor dog frown.
So I sleep and dream of fun
and romping in the noonday sun.
Then I wake and have my feed
and go out walkies on my lead.

It's dark outside with wind a howling
stopping creatures from their prowling.
Wind is gusting, trees are bending
blowing, blowing, never ending.
Blowing out my tidy ruffs
with those horrid gusty puffs!
This I really can't abide
so walk real close to Momma's side.
Leaves are whirling round my feet
littering up the tidy street.
Drops are dripping from the trees
blown down by this horrid breeze.
Twigs and puddles everywhere.
Tonight I'll say a little prayer
and ask Him if He'll send the sun
back, so His pets can have more fun!

Edna M Burns

MY DOG

To go into the house the dog looks fast asleep
From under those eyelids his crafty eyes do peep.
His eyes open up they open so wide
Within a few seconds he's right by your side.

He'll ask for some water he'll ask for some food
The way that he asks I'm sure it's not rude.
He'll give a little bark even shake his head
To jump up and down to make sure that he's fed.

When the cats see him coming their exit is fast
Because the way that he's running their lives just won't last.
They'll climb up a tree or jump over the gate
Even though this dog's fast he's always too late.

As a small treat he loves a ride in the car
We give him this treat because he doesn't go very far.
If the gate is left open he will start to roam
But we give him a whistle and he comes running home.

Dennis N Davies

THE VERY IDEA

I have a little doggie his name is Dirty Rick,
He does his pooh under the sideboard what a dirty trick,
My home I keep so spotless, as clean as a new pin,
I've tried everything that's possible, I simply cannot win
One day I had a brainwave, to stop his little act,
So I put it into practice, with diplomacy and tact,
But when I told my husband, he simply laughed and roared,
My idea simply had to work, I cut the legs off the sideboard.

Sylvia Lowe

THE SANCTUARY

I adopted a shire horse called Jessie
She was rescued from slaughter with her daughter
They're both safe from harm
To live their lives in calm
No one can do them any harm
They have many horses as friends
Albert, Henry, Rodney and Jack
They all don't mind if you ride on their back
They are so trusting and friendly
How can people be their enemy
To beat them and starve them
And send them to slaughter
Not even a drink of water
I'm glad there's a sanctuary to look after them
At least they can end their days
In their own precious ways
Munching on grass and oats
And special people to groom their coats.

Ann Smith

LOVE ALONE

Eyes of trust look back at me
Loyalty without comparison
A tender age yet suffered at the hand of man.
Ask for little and deserving more
Drift deep within those brown eyes
Mirror reflections of what man can do;
Move gently for fear of punishment
Lay tender hands on glossy coat
A new life to begin
Though still a long road of dreams
Quiet the creature, for it knows fear
Still the beast with love alone . . .

James Samuel Clarke

DEATH IN THE AFTERNOON

She runs along frantic lathered with sweat
As if she knows, her fate will be death
With horse and hounds forever gaining ground
No hiding place, can be found.

It was late afternoon, with a blood red sky
'Neath a mighty great oak, the vixen did die.
The pursuit had been long, by the men in red,
Who would never give up, until she was dead.

She sort refuge by the tree, as a last resort,
To be torn to pieces, in the name of sport,
Some say, this creature, is nothing but a pest,
But it's the hunting gentry, that should be lain to rest

John J Hudson

TRIXIE

I have a small dog
She's very old you see
No one else would take her in
as she's twenty three

She coughs and splutters
as she's very old
I bought her off a gypsy
and brought her in, out of the cold

She cost me five pounds
every penny I had
But I think she's worth it
even though she's bad

Lilian Coombs

ANTS' NEST

I lay myself bare; rays of summer sunshine dissolving inhibition,
freeing me to float upon the subtle sense of nature:
I gazed across at the hard baked earth,
where tufts of juicy green freshly sprouted, each delicately unique;
the stroke of a work of art that had taken aeons to create.

My mind increasingly focused on such intensity of detail;
each miniature stone and grain of dirt, patiently hand crafted;
suddenly my attention jumped, drawn by the flicker of movement:
an ant, most perfectly formed, wandered amongst the undergrowth;
my scope of sight expanded to reveal the numerous presence;
hundreds of ants, toing and froing, as one collective family,
each with definite purpose, working for the greater whole;
hypnotised in amazement I followed their individual paths;
accompanying hurried journeys, deciphering some meaning:
I was struck by lightning . . . caught in an earthquake . . .
my mind blown wide open and flooded with realisation:

Life in over-abundance was oozing from every pore of nature:
like a million echoing crickets on a starry summer's night,
with deafening reels of joy I heard the heavenly songs of creation;
every sense instantly bombarded:
a prowling cat pounced from camouflage bushes,
seagulls cried in glory gliding radiant updrafts,
thrushes chirped and chattered from the comforting arms of trees,
swifts danced and flirted with the sky,
bees bumbled on the warm rose-scented air,
a dragonfly hummed in and out of vision,
snails shaded on the undersides of leaves,
spiders hid, worms squirmed, beetles trekked, butterflies flowered . . .

It was a timeless moment of ecstasy, to which I now return;
life pulsating everywhere . . . if only we could see . . .

Jamie Best

WGAS RULE OKAY

I want to write a verse
But I have no time to rehearse
I want to help the WGAS
A much better cause than booze or fags
They take in animals that need a helping hand
And care for them on their special land
A place they sense they're safe to be
One that needs upkeeping by you and me
Where there are special people who really care
And with the animals their love they want to share
So anytime you have a little spare money
Remember the WGAS and let the animals too live on milk and honey
Thank you for reading my little small verse
Even though I had no time to rehearse

Cherry Somers-Dowell

BOO BOO

Our family started by adopting,
We got ourselves a stripey cat,
At first he was timid and nervous,
But soon, he had hung up his hat.
He soon became Lord of the household,
Telling us, with loud meows, he wants fed,
Then after playing all day, climbing curtains
He slept all night on his bed,
The RSPCA, did a good job,
In letting us take that cat home,
The poor little thing, was tired and thin,
And now, it no longer need roam,
We loved him so much, he was happy,
He was well fed, and cared for each day,
Thank you for letting us have him.
Our Boo Boo has now passed away.

Kazzie Ingram

MY BIG BALL OF FUR

I once had a dog called Lassie
She was big and brown and white
yes she had a temper
            So she'd guard my home each night
I had her from a baby
and she was faithful to her end
but she wasn't just my dog
She was also my best friend,
Then she took ill, with a cancer lump
to hear that word made my heart jump
who would I tell about my worries and strife
Lassie was my listener, she was my life
She was alright for a while, Then came the pain
I knew deep inside She didn't want to remain
Then the vet said it's time to let her go
but I couldn't let him, I loved her so
I took her home knowing it was the last time
I told her I loved her and I was glad she was mine
we talked about years gone by,
            And how we'd both grown
we talked about the future
            Now I'd be all alone
Then the next day they put her to sleep
all I could do was weep and weep
thirteen years together, right up to her end
            and when I lost Lassie
            I also lost my best friend
I've other pets now but I'll never forget her
            my lovely Lassie
            my big ball of fur

Heather Dunn-Fox

MY CAT

Woken by pat on nose as she taps with her paws
To awake from slumber, my cat
not like another, this white and grey, tapping away
Want milk or food, or both, go away
But No, she has her way.

I rise to the surface, is it work today?
Oh cat, please go away, I'm too tired to play.

She eats the fish, drinks the milk, then
goes out for a while whilst I stand by the sink,
watching her.
She hides from the dog, but braves other cats
that inhabit our street,
Sits on the wall, sunning herself,
and sleeps.

Come on cat, it's time to come in,
I'm going to work, late as it is,
You can sleep inside on the window sill

I'll see you tonight when I come home.

You'll be all alone, but that's alright
Dreaming cat's dream, and fighting cat's fight.

Closing door, starting car
Rush,rush, rush
Not very far

to the office, then

home again. What a day, what a day,
Come on little puss, wake up, wake up,
I'm home from work, and it's time to play.

Margaret Crabtree

PANTHERA TIGRIS

Gleaming eyes that shine so bright,
They stare, peering through the night.
Sinews rippling o'er calcium rich bone,
As its journey it continues alone.
Silent paws padding on jungle ground,
A graceful movement, ne'er making a sound.
Colour, markings a beautiful face.
Disguises its shape with every pace.
Through the forest that is so thick,
It travels slow and sometimes quick,
That a flash is oft all that's seen.
With a sense of smell so very keen.
A creature much maligned by man,
He'll ignore you if he can.
Gleaming eyes that shine so bright.
As it travels on into night.

Josie Minton

EAGLE SONG

Flying above the trees
On the early morning breeze
My darling rising eagle
Flying up above
Look down on us humans
Bless us all with love
Fly above us calling
Trying to tell us all
How mighty is the river
And rushing waterfall .
You are up above
We are down below
How much I want to be with you
No-one can ever know

Yvonne Dickinson

CATS

Cats are really beautiful
So stately and serene,
So graceful and mischievous,
And hardly ever mean.

They'll balance most precariously
Upon a fence so narrow,
Then spot a mouse or bird to chase
And shoot off like an arrow.

They always choose the sunny spots
In the garden when it's fine
And when the winter winds do blow
The warmest place they'll find.

Cats really are a breed apart,
Aloof and yet so knowing,
They purr like engines when they're pleased
But beware, when claws are showing.

Their eyes are just like jewels
Of blue, brown green or gold
Their fur so sleek and shiny
A pleasure to behold.

When you come home, you'll always get
A welcome, warm as toast
(Or could it be the meat they smell
That you've brought home to roast?)

Whatever makes them lovely,
For lovely's what they are,
It's great to have a cat around
-The most perfect pet by far.

Janet Boor

THE SUPERIOR RACE

The seal swims effortlessly in the sea,
its perfected lines are sleek.
This world's a wonderful place to be,
doesn't it make you feel really meek.

The whale is a gentle creature,
magnificent in its gait.
The best created by nature,
yet conjuring up feelings of hate.

The gorilla is really shy and warm,
hiding deep in the jungle.
It usually only comes out at dawn,
doesn't it make you feel humble?

The humans are the superior race,
with so much to see and enjoy.
Why can't we open our arms and embrace,
instead of being set to destroy?

Why is this world so complicated,
shattered dreams with so much hatred.
Why do we feel the need to kill,
how long will it take to reach our fill.

Sue Stierer

TO A BLACKBIRD

Blackbird, Blackbird
You're such a happy fellow
With your feathers so black
Your beak so yellow

Blackbird, Blackbird
On the highest bough
You sing your song, from morn to night
As happy as the day, is long and light.

Blackbird, Blackbird
You fill our world
With pure delight
You are such a lovely sight.

Blackbird, Blackbird
From my window, I watch you sing
A touch of joy, to this world you bring
So sing your heart out, pretty bird,
I will watch, without a word.

Irene Corbett

CARLOS THE CAT

A cat curled sleeping
A soft, warm ball
Comforting
As it lies
Innocent
From the world
A rhythmic purr
That doesn't pause
But gently hums
Along
Magnificent paws extended
Buzzing body sings
A song
Majestic
In its feline grace
Leaps and circles
Dances
With eyes that
Light
A darkened room
A glittery gleam
As it pounces

Miriam Eissa

MINNIE THE DORMOUSE
(Dedicated to my daughter Rita-Michaela)

Remember, all the tiny woodland creatures,
That live at the bottom of trees!
They strive to survive, no matter
What the weather, rain or shine,
Through all the frost, snow, draught, all year round!

As we enjoy the comfort and warmth of a cosy fire,
Minnie, the dormouse strives to survive!
Scurrying around all day long, until late at night,
Trying to gather hazelnuts, with all her skill.
And sweet honeysuckle bark to line her nest, until dark.

Minnie, must not be careless and seen out late,
Else she becomes prey, to owls, she hates!
In her cosy nest, lined with honeysuckle bark
Deep in her burrow, near the old oak tree,
Sheltered from weather, and the strange invader!

This tiny creature, with her two beady-black eyes
Beautiful reddish coat and bushy tail,
If you meet her, very shy, she doubts all passers-by!
When the days are short and cold or wet,
She retires to sleep, cuddled up to her mate!

When the ravages of winter, are all around,
Minnie and her mate, are burrow bound,
They live on the food gathered at harvest time
Meagre it may be, but it must last
Feed all her family until the winter is past.

Then when Spring is knocking on the door
They all emerge, proud, having survived once more
Constantly living in fear, as the owls sear
Minnie and her offspring, down the cove disappear!
Remember! These tiny creatures have first claim
To the woodlands, it is their home, where they live and roam!

Anna Elliott

LOVE RETURNED

Rustie dear Rustie young and spritely
Brown coat gleaming as she sprinted
Up the stairs and down again
Across the fields and along the shores
Just a little brown pup then she was
We loved her dearly she knew that
Her adoring eyes brown and shining
Would look at her master and knew to obey
A kiss a cuddle a rub down
Tummy rubbed fur smoothed down
A piece of fudge a fresh bone
Oh yes she knew she was loved
Her walk grows slower now
The change from a pup to ageing years
Have flown past it seems untrue
We will always have our memories
To keep for ever more

Lily Robinson

ANIMAL LOVERS

Do treat your pet with care,
Because they don't ask to be there.

They cannot talk,
But like to be taken for a walk.

Give them little treats,
And nice meats.

Keep them clean,
Then they are fit to be seen.

Rita Rogers

TIG

If I cried a million tears today
So my Tig could see the snow
I know my tears would be in vain
So I'll guide you where you go.

Your two brown eyes no longer see
You only hear a dove,
But Tig there's one thing that's for sure
You were raised on lots of love.

If I was granted one wish
I know what it would be
I'd say 'Please bless my baby's eyes,'
And you would let him see.

Shirley Chapman

UNTITLED

Oh little Chinese crested
       with your head up in the sky,
he watches every move
       and asks no reason why.
he has a dainty little walk
       and the courage of a king,
no-one understands that
       he fears not anything.

Oh little Chinese crested
       who is, oh so very wise,
you can see his world within
       when you look into his eyes.
To people he is cheeky
       especially for his size.
He is simply made of good things
       a heaven in disguise.

Alison Taylor

CHANCE OF A LIFE

Cats are old hat,
But most of us love 'em.

They tease us, appease us
and rake at our legs.
They love us, they cuddle us,
use us as beds.

What more could you ask
from these bundles of joy
stalked out that mouse,
for your use as a toy?

No fear in their eyes
So content in this life
No worries of starvation
Of trouble and strife.

And lucky for those
For there are some who are not
Dumped without food
In a world left to rot.

And desperate are they
for the chance to survive,
A little care, a little love
And the chance of a life.

Andrew Jones

A FRIEND FOREVER

We have a dog named Jodie
My daughter and I
She has so many winning ways
She is very loyal and loving
Everyone who sees her
Would like her for their own
Her stomach's always rumbling
Food she very much enjoys
One of her favourite treats is walkies
It's a special part of her day
Also she loves her special comforts
Like lying by the fireside
and getting on the bed
She really gets quite spoilt
But we wouldn't have it any other way
When she leaves this world
as one day she surely will
She will be greatly missed
But memories will always be with us
of all the happiness she gave
and those no-one can take away

Pam Jewell

FRIENDS

Relaxing in my armchair on cold winter nights,
Sharing the warm fire light with my feline friend,
I feel the silence around us like velvet on silk,
Both not wanting this tranquil time to end.

Many long years you have hypnotised me,
With your bright eyes looking deep into my soul,
You know all my secrets, my joys, my heart aches,
But alas your feelings and thoughts I know not at all.

Always doing things your way, proud and independent,
But as you grow older you need me more,
And if I seem to forget you on busy days,
You remind me by catching the hem of my dress with a paw.

When I pick you up and cuddle you close,
Your body seems so fragile and small,
But underneath that fur of midnight black,
Beats the heart of a warrior bold.

Dawn Shaw

FRIENDLY PETS

We once had a golden Labrador
The most docile dog we ever saw
He grew to be quite a size
Very friendly and very wise
More like a horse to our young son
Sat on his back loved by everyone
A softy with mournful eyes
Would look down at the cats in surprise
As they crept slowly up to steal
And help themselves to his favourite meal
This Golden Labrador we had for years
The cats get killed which ended in tears
They hunted by night slept during the day
Would kill the mice but kept the moles at bay
We had a large lawn all smooth and green
No mole hills were ever seen
Sooty our favourite we thought was lost for good
We were later to find he'd been trapped in a wood
He returned after several days tired and thin
Dragging a snare attached to him
He was the most agile cat of all
Good as a squirrel at spanning a wall

Doris Tyler

BEAR

Oh, the folly
of wayward humans,
as they after pleasure seek
to inflict their domination
on animals.
Usurping nature's balance,
their jollity to make.
As the bears stumble
to the dance of death
with their muzzled, ringed nose
exuding pain; they laugh.
Oh the suffering it feels
from barbaric handlers;
extracting glee
from onlooking tourists
keen to view.
Whose is the ultimate wickedness,
the doers,
or those who come to see?

Ted Harrison

ANIMAL CARE

We have a message to bring you
Of God's creatures here on earth
Which He created and placed in our keeping
And how He considers great their worth.

For the comfort they so often give us
When we're alone or with family.
Of joint pleasure with those that are roaming
For whose birthright it is to live free.

But how humankind abuses them,
What pain they often inflict.
We're therefore so thankful for all of those
Who take care of the injured and sick.

Thank God for His animal nation.
Thank God for those people who care.
Let's hope this caring of God's wondrous creation
Will one day fill all hearts everywhere.

Martine L Shelton

DEATH OF A DEER

The light and glow in her large dewy eyes
Grows dim and dull as she gently dies.
The rifle cracked and the bullet sped
The wound was fatal the wound it bled.
The ground grew scarlet the blood did flow
Death came swiftly to this graceful doe.
The rays of the sun lit the glade in the morning,
Sparkling the dew as the day was dawning.
The soft melody of the song birds singing,
Set the woodland air there ringing
Squirrels pranced in the soft green leaves
Which were stirring gently with a fragrant breeze
Rabbits grazed in the glade below
By a trickling stream with a bubbling flow
Then the crack of the shot split the air around
The velvet soft deer slid to the ground
Silence came like a blanket of snow
The life blood ebbed from the eyes of the doe
The creatures fled in the morning dew
The deer lay still her last breath she drew.
How could he do this deed he has done?
Will God forgive this man with a gun?

Sue Saxby

THE DOLPHIN

The dolphin came an hour ago
when the fog was thick and choking
as the ferry quietly journeyed
from Lerwick down to Stromness.

Our minds were blank in thought
as we wore out the panelled decks
with tiredness in our eyes
and frustration in our hearts.

The silence was our foe
and the visionless surroundings
with five hours yet to pass
before our journey's close.

Then she appeared below
to travel by our side
surfacing here and there
helping us on our way.

I strengthen in her guide
yet wonder deep inside
if I joined her in her home
would she stop and play a while.

Mark Baine

SAM

First thing every morning you rush into my bed
You lie next to me and I gently stroke your head

Then off we go for your daily run to the park
But first you must have a run around and a little bark

The next ritual is that you must be fed
Then off you go and take yourself back to bed

When I come home from work you are always there to greet me
Your little tail wagging so enthusiastically

Then later in the evening when we settle to watch the telly
You roll over onto your back so I can tickle your belly

You have got such sad eyes and a beautiful face
No dog in the world could ever take your place

I love you very much and I know you love me too
I am very lucky to have a special friend like you.

Carol M Deakin

ANIMAL

Tawny and Snowy perch, a pair relaxing in the trees at the
moment, this year safe in the knowledge that nature has been
kind, generous, defined.
Either of the barn or the field, the earth or the water nature
created the animals from before God's rebirth.

On all fours or on the wing like a little bird that joyously
sings the animals of this world enhance our lives.
From Butch the dog to Kitty the cat, or the little mouse in
the house to the big fat rat, the animals are here it's a fact
at that.

Majestic lions proud and strong prowl Africa's lands every morn.
The fish in the seas are many varied learning in schools,
and swimming far from tides.
Dolphins, whales, sharks watch them glide.
The Ants outnumber us 1 million to one, or so I hear.
But we share this earth beneath the sun, I like these animals
one and all and beside them all we stand tall.

Kieran Rafferty

JACK RUSSELL

Not tall of size or short of courage
not slow to warn of strangers at the door
your ears are sharp when mine are dim
your friendship true even when all others
forget to show their love but not you.
Though many dogs there may be yes and
some with long pedigrees, many dogs
may win at Crufts some dogs may be
very tough some may win a race others
be of fine grace.
But of all the dogs I am glad I chose you
for no other dog could be a friend so true
Never grumbles never moans always glad
to see me home, never worried never
ruffled when you have a friend in a
Jack Russell.

Reg Cooper

ALL CREATURES GREAT AND SMALL

I've handled many animals with tender loving care,
The experiences of which I hope that you will share,
There's been penguins and ducks that have gone to far off places,
Dogs, cats and rabbits with the cutest of faces,
A parrot with colourful feathers, lots of bumbly bees,
So that the act of my devotion everybody sees,
Now elephants of all sizes don't bother me a jot,
Bears, polar bears, and a panda I've coped with on the spot,
A blue whale has passed through my hands, and so have a few mice,
To stare a lion in the face some folk would not think twice,
Disabled on horseback, that's to whom I devote my craft,
I'll carry on till my hands pack up, no one thinks me daft,
I've knit two owls, and sheep, and many other things as well,
What gives me immense pleasure, the look on their faces tell.

Joan Bowes

THE FAITHFUL FRIEND

A man's voice called his children in for tea,
Gathering them into his arms, talking gently,
With smiling eyes and huge, protective hands,
His kind face expressed all the love he felt,

He told a story of the dog he had when a boy,
How much he and his family had loved the pet,
Then came the day, just before Christmas Eve,
This beloved animal had suddenly disappeared.

His joy was over-shadowed by the missing pet,
As he went in search of her calling her name,
Scouring each inch of ground on the hillside,
The tears springing up into his eyes in grief,

Turning to go home, utterly dejected and sad,
Feeling desolate at what the loss would mean,
Suddenly he was aware of something moving,
Kneeling, cupped in his hands a new-born pup.

Astonished, he heard other whimpering sounds,
His gaze followed the cries to other puppies
As they lay snuggling in the nest of bracken
With their proud mother, his faithful friend.

Almost dark by now, he must go to fetch help
To bring the pups and their mother back home.
Checking they were comfortable, he left them,
His mind marvelling at the miracle of nature.

When the father finished recounting this story
Of the Christmas long ago from his childhood,
The magic that Christmas had meant much more,
This message he conveyed to his children now.

Betty Mealand

THE OCEAN AND OTHERS WHERE WE SHOULD GIVE PEACE

If we are to find the depths of our soul,
To the bed of the ocean we should go,
There we will find so many treasures,
A heavenly light shines through its pleasures,
As we listen we find many secrets,
Things long forgotten with many regrets,
The sea will give up so many things,
We only need to look and listen,
As the waves of love and beauty glisten,
It holds the Whales and Dolphins with spirit so grand,
If only us humans could understand,
All that these creatures hold in their soul,
Their secrets they will give to those who know,
How to receive and understand,
There are souls such as these in every land,
Souls that are sent to lighten the world,
One day for sure their secrets will unfurl.

The father God holds each in his hand,
Whether or not you understand,
To each soul He gives a home,
According to how you have learned to grow,
Then each will find their rightful place,
Perhaps not always to their previous grace,
But every house that is built above,
Is poor of mansion of God's great love,
And if you give to others in need,
You will find a blessed home,
In Spirits' Land of Peace,
So good people on this God's Land,
Remember the day and I'm sure you will understand,
The Good Lord Jesus came among us to show us a way,
Treat all with respect and Love Untold,
On Land and Sea and things will Surely Unfurl.

Michael J Taylor

A DREAM COME TRUE

A lifelong ambition was realised when I was thirty-seven,
The one thing I had always prized, at last in my possession.
Since I was only two years old I'd plagued my Mum and Dad,
Year after year I'd be told it's just a passing fad.
I knew they could not afford one and tried to understand,
Going short of nothing else, the subject would be banned.
I learned to ride the hard way and worked at a riding school,
Happy as a sandboy, stubborn as a mule.
Years later, settled with children, the dream was still as strong,
Riding lots of other people's, never having one of my own.
Then one day, quite by chance, it seems that fate stepped in,
I chanced upon an advert, briefly describing Him,
Leaving a note for my husband, off I set on the bus,
'Gone to look at a horse dear,' thinking how he would fuss.
I hadn't any money but that was easily solved,
I thought it was quite funny, and so the plot evolved.
The handsome beast was Coco, neurotic and so thin,
He'd got away with murder and thought he'd always win.
Now, I quite like a challenge, so decided to give him a try,
He did his best to ditch me, reared up then shot off for miles.
Well, panicked but never beaten, I had to take him in hand,
A chat at the bank, he was delivered and years of pleasure began.
I loved that horse to pieces, he soon became my friend,
But I progressed and he didn't so he had to go in the end.
I cried for hours that dreadful day, it almost broke my heart,
We'd been so good for each other, but now it was time to part.
He'd given me back my confidence and so much pleasure of course,
There'll always be a special place in my heart for my first horse.

Linda Cannings

MY OLD FAITHFUL FRIEND

When my family's too busy,
And my friends just don't care,
I talk to my dog,
For he's always there.
I tell him my worries,
My hopes and my fears,
He listens with interest,
Or so it appears.
He sits there beside me
When I'm in my chair,
Just watching and dozing,
He's quite happy there.
He's totally indifferent
To what's on TV,
He's just quite contented
To be there with me.
And even when I'm
All alone in my bed,
I can stretch out my hand
And feel his soft head.
I think he is all that
A good friend should be;
Thank you, my friend,
For coming to me.

Heather Sims

EYES I REMEMBER

The wide blue eyes of my mother
    As she crouched beneath the stair
As German bombs came screaming down
    Around us everywhere

The eyes of my new born sister
    Of the deepest violet hue
While each of her five elder sisters
    Had either hazel or blue

The striking eyes of a young lad
    In shirt of turquoise blue
As he leant against the fish shop wall
    For his eyes were turquoise too.

The dark brown eyes of a lovely girl
    As she left the cottage small
On the arm of the man she loved
    Her eyes just said it all

But the eyes that most impress me
    Are not human eyes at all,
They belong to a rough coated mongrel
    Rescued when she was small.

I do not see her often
    But always when I do
Her soft brown eyes are laughing
    And I find I'm laughing too.

Pauline G Gillham

THE RIVER THE ANIMALS SAVED

The river was long and winding,
Like a silvery snake twisting
Through fields and forests
'Til winter's ice came misting.

Then the stretching river froze over -
Time stood still under its cover
And all around in its wintry glory
Trees and meadows from nature's mother.

Birds sang songs to break the ice,
Sung about valleys and all things nice,
Even the hedgehogs woke from their slumber
All joined in, including the mice.

High in the sky the sun sat shining,
Warming the ice 'til it started declining
From the river's water and the bushes and trees,
And droplets of ice to the ground started sliding.

The water began once more to run
And creatures from afar started to come
To listen to the story of how they'd all
Chased away Jack Frost and the battle they'd won.

G Robson

THE SWAN

Silently floating, whiter than lace
Gliding along with beauty and grace
The swan is approaching at leisurely pace

The water reflecting her image so fine
She seems to be regardless of time
From some other world, God's garden may be
To give us a glimpse, of just what could be

Majestic in sunlight, or moon's silvery glow
Hardly a ripple from her as she goes
A creation so perfect, she swims on and on
This wonderful queen of the water - the swan

Dennis Curley

BELLISSIMA

The day after Epiphany
When snow was on the ground
She came to join our family
Excitement all around

>We loved her from the very start
>But she would bide her time
>Before she'd take us to her heart
>Her feelings so sublime

She sat there graceful and serene
Her presence filled the room
A blonde - a Persian Beauty Queen
With tail of ambered plume

>Hard to believe she was a stray
>With nobody to care
>But we adored her from that day
>Bellissima - so fair

She brought us so much ecstasy
We had to name her Bliss
Enriched our lives so purrfectly
A special cat is this

Arlene Skerratt

TALISMAN

My hot water bottle
sings me to sleep
and protects me
from the night time creatures
that drool near the bed.

In the morning
she wakes me
with careful kisses
and a sigh,
then stands on my head
and demands to be fed.

Add during the day
with effulgent eyes
that twitch to the dances of birds
she misses nothing
but watches patient
for my return.

A shout,
through a white puff of stream,
as she leaps to my arms
and welcomes me home.

Benjamin F Jones

SANDY

Oh! My poor paws, they're so sore today
Walking around trying to find my prey
Under the bushes - up in the trees
I can't even find a mouse to tease

If I stay still, and not make a sound
That bird that's flying round and round
Might land - and feed without a care
Not knowing that I'll be waiting there

Look out! Here comes another tom cat
Soaking wet - he looks like a rat
He's spoilt my chance of an early tea
I'd better get home - no prey for me.

Christine Thain

NOT A MODEL PUSS

In padded basket softly lined
A little kitten I did find;
From generous Aunt my kitten came,
So small, so fragile, yet so tame,
With coat of furry white, quite clean,
And gleaming black with silken sheen,
With tabby paws with which it walked,
And ears which listened as we talked,
With greeny eyes so wide with fright
With which it saw so clear at night.
But from that little kitten sweet,
In padded basket, soft and neat,
There grew a heart so fierce and strong,
A mind that always thought of wrong.
When children stroked his glossy fur
Expecting him to turn and purr
He showed his fiery teeth and jaws,
And scratched at them with tabby paws.
With other cats my pet would fight
And steal their food when out of sight,
And then at eve, the end of day,
My cat upon the rug would play,
But when a new home we did find
Stayed at the home we left behind.

Margaret E Turtle

WOMAN'S BEST FRIEND

Those big brown eyes stare back at me
Little dog you must be ready for tea
We've had lots of fun just me and her
She rolled in mud, just look at her fur,
I'll have to brush her, clean her paws
Or there'll be marks on all the floors,
There, miracles are performed with a brush and comb
All nicely groomed for her return home,
I'll miss her for certain but a long stay she's had
Saying goodbye is always quite sad
So go into your basket you bundle of fun
You bring so much pleasure by the ton!

Janet Bedford

PET SHOP

It was such a magical place,
The pet shop in the market place,
Smells of the farmyard waft in the air,
Quickening the senses of wolds and lanes,
Crowded with people from everywhere,
Even city slickers in bowler hats,
Children mesmerised with the parrots' chats
Cute little puppies looking forlorn,
All they need is a loving home,
A little old lady took up their plight,
Cuddle the puppy and it was plain to see
They were intended for one another,
To fill the empty need,·
She had found a faithful friend,
The puppy a loving home.

Janet Burton Taylor

BRANDED BEFORE TRIED

Your fur
is so silky.
Yet you look
so rough.
Your nature
is soft and cuddly,
but you're branded
as tough.
People don't see
the real you.
Reading their local papers
is all they do.
If they really showed
any interest,
they'd all know
that I am the one
who loves you.

Sue Harrison

BRITTLE BIRDSONG

Walking beside garden trilling;
Walking under seagull shrilling;
Imagining effortless flight-thrilling;
Layer of hedgerow birds - lull of birdsong.
Strata of darting martins shriek of wrong
The Devil's Messengers with high pitch screech
That the stormy seagulls hope to drown. Reach
My soul to the height of hawk and kestrel.

The beauty of the beast that silent fell
On the breathlessness of brittle birdsong

Suzanne Stratful

121

MY DOG, MY FRIEND

I'm all alone
My friend has
Gone
With all this
Loneliness
Can I carry on?

The walks we
Shared
The memories
Still there
I expect you
To be lying
By my chair.

The years of fun
And being together
They're the ones
I'll always treasure

But now you're gone
The house is bare
For you, my friend
You're no longer
There

But one day
We'll be together
And go on in life
Not death
Forever

Amanda J Silver

SIEGFRIED

I remember the day I saw him first
a bundle of black fur, caked in dirt
abandoned by people who didn't care
left with the rubbish to die right there
but two young girls who saw his plight
carried him home to me that night
a scrap so small and so alone
badly needing a nice kind home
I named him Siegfried and loved him so
but God loved him too and he had to go
back to his home beyond the sky
back to his maker up on high
I miss him still and hope that he
one day will be waiting for me
then never again will I be apart
from the kitten I love with all my heart.

Shirley E Faulkner

LUKE AND FRIENDS

My name is Luke, my friends Mongey, Brat and me
We were once in an animal shelter you will see
We had no special human to see to our needs
Take us for long walks, give us special feeds
Then one day Animal Aid came to take us for a walk
And with my sad expression, it was as if I could talk
The people I now live with fell to my charms
Took me to live on their small animal friendly farm
We are altogether my two friends and me
I will leave this here, as it is time for my tea.

Melanie M Burgess

123

LEAH

King or Princess her title implies
though to me she's both and more,
black as night, shining stars her eyes
her whole being I love and adore.
Elusive, mysterious, her history unknown
she brought when she entered my life,
thin and ill-treated her frame hardly grow
what cruelty have you seen? What strife?
Escaped, abandoned her face wildly shone
fear not, forget, your past is now gone.

Will Shakespeare cry at the name she now holds
what the title implies, its expectations
fear not dear William, there's no need to scold
for she will lift your heart with elation.
But no Cordelia she'll bear, no Gonerill or Regan
for tis too risky in our kingdom's state,
because creatures need care and love to lean on
please don't grieve my dear Queen of Spades.
Does your mind ever drift to motherhood gone?
Forgive me my Princess, play on, play on.

Your ignorant bliss I covert and envy
for knowledge brings sadness and fears,
now that you're safe the love is in plenty
though many like you still shed tears.
Dream sweetly my pup as you lay by the grate
for the world's still a beautiful place,
if only they'd stop their cruelty and hate
with just a look from your face.
King and Princess your title implies
though to me you're more, much more in my eyes.

Andrea Fairweather

THERE'S THE DONKEYS, DAD!

The tide is coming in and I am glad,
For soon no longer will I have to stand
While children's sticky hands ungloss my coat,
And I survey this endless stretch of sand.

Those upturned faces round the ice-cream van
Confirm my deep and overwhelming fears.
With dripping cones they'll rush to be the first
To rub my nose and backward bend my ears.

They'll clamber up and choke me with the reins,
While Dad with camera crouches on one knee,
'Head up, hold on, yes look I'm over here,
A big smile now. That's it. 'Does he mean me?

But wait! A rumour is around that there's a home,
A Donkey Sanctuary I'm told it's called,
A place of quiet retirement, peace and calm,
With single stalls together with full board.

I'm dreaming now of how I'll spend each day,
Maybe I'll breakfast 'neath my favourite tree,
And then I'll take a turn around the field
To pass the time of day with folks like me.

They say I'll miss the sand, the sea, the smells,
The sound of screeching dodgems on the pier,
But when I stretch and yawn and doze again
I'll have no yearning thoughts - *Wish you were here.*

May Webb

125

THE LAB

I was once a little rabbit, living in a wood.
Happy and carefree life was so good.
One day a man took me, he wouldn't let me go,
I wondered what was happening, but then I didn't know.

I was taken to the dungeon, also known as the Lab.
It is not exactly a holiday, *in fact it is really bad.*
Next day I was taken out, chemicals dropped in my eye,
Nobody tried to help me, and no one heard me cry.

Next a burning substance is forced into my nose.
My back was used to test lotion that smelled just like a rose
Then I was put in a furnace, to see the affect on my skin.
They carefully shaved off my fur I fought but had to give in.

Now they have finished, they have put me on Death Row.
Tomorrow I'll be put to sleep, in case you didn't know.
I'd just like to tell about the rabbits' plight,
I'd like someone to help us, when you read this you might.

All this pain we have to suffer, we rabbits aren't so tough,
So please buy cruelty free products animals have suffered enough.

Janine Fox (14)

MAN'S BEST FRIEND

My dog is small and is my pal
Helping me through life, somehow.
Every day when I get home
I take him out and we're alone.

We travel here, we travel there,
Seeing all without a care.
Life's too short and soon could end
We all need 'man's best friend'.

Marian Lloyd

FOR MY DOG

We've spent many years together,
You and I, my friend,
And now it seems that one of us,
Is facing his life's end.

How can I tell you how much,
Your love has meant to me,
Your trust and your devotion,
And unfailing loyalty.

You've always been there for me,
You've always thought I'm best,
And no matter what has happened,
Your love has stood the test.

But though we have to part,
It's not forever you see,
For when I get to heaven I know,
You'll be there waiting for me.

Shirley Lloyd

SCRATCH THE CAT

I was given a black cat
I was told my luck would change,
So I called him Lucky.
Hoping he would chase the mice away,
But all he wanted to do was play,
This black cat was so untrue.
He crawled at the wall and scrawled
up the door, that's it I thought.
So I changed his name and called him Scratch.
Hoping then he would send the mice on their way
but it was not to be as he is still playing
with the mice today.

Tracy Salt

BEFORE IT IS TOO LATE

From the swans on Tschaikowsky's Lake
To the spider in the bath,
In the future all have a stake
And are part of the aftermath.
From the elephant so huge and grey
So gentle and yet strong,
To the seals that swim in a Devon bay
In trust to us all belong.
To betray that trust will seal our fate,
What we sow we shall surely reap.
We must not kill what we cannot create
Or the kraken will wake from the deep.
At nature we cringe with contempt
When it's red in tooth and claw,
But they only kill with a need to pre-empt
Where the rule of the jungle is law.
We use them for gratification,
How we look, what we eat, what we wear,
No thought for their sensation,
Will no one ever care?
How long must we be so blind,
On nature force our will,
They only ask us to be kind,
Their fearful hearts to still.
I look into my spaniel's eyes
And see the love that is there,
Then I know it is time to be as wise
And warn the world - 'Take care'.

Bernadette Bryant

128

MY HORSE (HOLLY)

My horse is not just a horse, he is my friend as well you know!
I love him so dearly and trust him so
He is patient and kind and always ready to go
He comes when he is called with a loud whinny and high kick
He never ever, needs a stick,
He has a lovely big stable, where he is happy to be
or out in the fields when not riding with me,
I very happily 'muck out'
and my Mum says, spend hours messing about,
I feed him and tend him, his hooves pick out
I brush him with care, until his coat shines bright
Go to his stable last thing every night
put on his rug and say with a hug, 'night night'
I love him so much, I just have to see that he is alright

We ride across the moss every day, come what may
Done a great many miles in our day
We love the sun, the wind and the rain
Often get wet, change and go out again
Even if the snow, we still love to go

We really enjoy doing a show, and usually win when we go!
We have hundreds of rosettes,
Silver cups and plaques, we like to collect

When you have 'Horse Love' in your blood
It is quite understood
It comes to stay, and never ever goes away

My 'Friend' and I love and trust each other
Many happy hours we spend together
There is nothing like the feel of a horse beneath you
Blissfully riding along . . . like we do.

Edna Parrington

TIM, MY FAITHFUL FRIEND

My faithful friend has wavy black hair
With a patch of white and golden-ringed eyes.
During the day, downstairs he mainly stays,
But at night, upstairs, on the spare bed he lies.
He is taken for a walk at least twice a day
And sometimes, if he is lucky, he'll see a friend and play.
He's warm and affectionate and mainly good as gold,
But sometimes he has a stubborn streak
And just will not do as he is told.
He's loving and forgiving, loyal and gentle too,
I love him very much, truly I do.
He's there every night greeting me with a friendly face
After I've spent a day at work in the hectic rat race.
He looks at me with his gorgeous brown eyes
As if to say, 'I love you Mum, thank you for giving me a loving home.'
For you see, my faithful friend is my dog, Tim
Who from an animal rescue centre he did come.

Lesley Stevenson

BILLIE BEAN SPROUT

Faithful friend
Sitting eyes agog
Lead tightly clenched
Crafty dog

Radar ears
Listening for the word
To spring to life
When 'walkies' is heard

Greyhound frame
Racing the track
Remote in the distance
Just a sighting in black

Pertinacious mutt
Ambitious scout
Enjoyable moment
With my Billie bean sprout.

Jane C Cook

IT'S A DOG'S LIFE

She's been hours dusting, the hoovering's done,
All of the washing's hanging out in the sun
I've chased the cats out of the garden, plus the odd bird or two,
If she's going to be much longer, I'll start chewing her shoe!

She's reaching for her coat and gloves, now that's a better sign,
Now on goes the welly boots, it really must be time
My lead is on, the door is locked, I'm ready for some fun
So come on Mum, let's set off, I'm ready for my run.

All those lovely sniffs and smells, going up the lane
I wonder if that nosey fox, will be on the ridge again,
We're up on the hill, now I can run free,
Julie Andrews has got nothing on me!

Down in the valley, the rabbits are basking I know
I start to give chase, but they all seem to go
It's sunny and warm now, I can't hang around though
I really must jump into, my favourite cow trough!

So fresh as a daisy, I run to Mum, and then shake
She's telling me off, did I make a mistake?
Once home, I shall have time, for a quick dream or two
Before Mum's produced, my most favourite stew.

Dorothy Cox

POLLY

Polly is my little cat
With fur as soft as cotton
She likes to climb up high in the trees
And there she plonks her bottom!

Polly cries when she is down
And grins when she is glad
Most of the time she is so good
But sometimes she is bad.

We spoil her rotten, I do think
As she always has her way
But I am here to comfort her
When bright days turn to grey.

She purrs her song so sweet to me
And a cuddle is her reward
I would love to play all day with her
But she goes to sleep and I'm bored.

I love my little Polly cat
And I think she loves me too
However much I tease her so
We stick like superglue!

Polly is my little cat
I would not want another
For I am Polly's little kit
And she is my second mother!

Jenny Amery

MOOR PONIES

Ponies grazing on the moors
Misty, raining, wind-swept moors
They don't seem to mind the weather
Bracing up against the heather.

Manes are flowing in the breeze
Some are sheltering in the trees
All the mares and foals to graze
In the moors mid-winter haze.

A filly foal with perfect star
Frolics with her kin
She knows not what the 'outside's' like
Sheltered from within.

But, once a year the humans come
And start a massive drive
Yearlings, colts, and filly foals
Will they all survive?

So colts, and fillies have your fun
While you are young and pure
Before too long the men will come
And break you in for sure . . .

Sylvia Fisher

EBONY

Little black cat so small and thin
Those stupid people shut you in
With two big cats who filled your life
With pain and misery and strife.

Little black cat only three months old
Siamese cats full grown and bold
Their teeth like needles, claws like knives
You had intruded in their lives.

Little black cat you were alone
They didn't want you in their home
They stole your food, tormented you
Their hatred shone from eyes ice blue.

Little black cat so wild and rough
You grew up mean, you grew up tough
You learnt to steal, you learnt to fight
You learnt to hate, you learnt to bite.

Little black cat so small and frail
You need no longer spit and growl
No longer do you have to fight
To eat your fill, it's yours by right.

Little black cat you're purring now
To love and trust you're learning how
Your nightmare is all finished with
You'll learn to play, you'll learn to give.

Little black cat laze up that tree
Those stupid people set you free
Your life no longer filled with fear
Your new mistress holds you dear.

Megan Owen

BLACK AND TAN

To Godmanchester we came to view
Confronted by animals of different sizes and hue
When one dog decided to leave the packs
Up to a grassy mound she made tracks
Although mainly a tan labrador she has the mask of an alsation
Which makes for far more fascination
'She's for us' we said assertively
So Karmen was taken for a walk with the family

Coming down in the dark of night
She shies away as I turn on the light
With a smile and a wag she screws up her eyes
Which seem to say: 'What a time to rise'
But as soon as she realises food is around
She is up with a leap and a bound

Now for the first treat of the day
Walkies in the fields with a chance to lead her furry friends astray
She races around with the wind up her tail
Sniffing here, bounding there, then lost on a scented trail

She lives with another dog you see
Intelligent wise and bright is little black Cherie
Contrived between them to shatter the calm
Of my gardening, each would pop a head under my arm
All collapsing in a heap a-laughing I would brace
Myself against a barrage of licks to my face

Kippers had been eaten for our tea
The skin of which was now free
To offer to Karmen whose eyes are bright
Intensity of which are like a search light
Ears pricked up, body quivering and mind eager
In anticipation she dribbles as I lower the tit bit to feed her

Diana Billett

135

SMUDGE

Smudge our dear black and white cat
despite his greed is not fat!
He is now getting on in years
and I fear there may soon be tears.
I recall him first as a ball of fur,
crouching under a living room chair.
He inveigled himself into our lives
with his daring mischievous ducks and dives.
His appetite was always amazing
for such a small half Burmese being.
It has often caused me to wonder
if we have a bulimic monster!
But in his many poses he is endearing
especially by the fire in the evening.
Our feline friend is losing his hair,
if this goes on what will he wear?
This cat with a black smudge on his nose,
which is his distinguishing feature,
is such an adorable creature.
O how we will miss watching you doze!

Heather Horlock

TOO CRUEL

You have to be cruel to be kind they say
but some people are cruel kindness not being there way
take people who are cruel to our four legged friends
they do not care if the pain never ends

Every day we see pictures which chill our bones
when pets are left starving and alone
there are people who would care for them
it seems their job will never end

Who could leave something crying in pain
and watch it suffer again and again
to me it would be just like leaving a child
when I think of such things my heart just goes wild

What made the world such a cruel place
and animals find hatred in the human face
we should live in a world of kindness I know
and our love of animals should always show

Maureen Lord

DADDY'S DOG

We've seen so much together,
Been through it side by side.
At times I've had to close my eyes.
While you've been my blind man's guide.
When I'm full of mixed emotions,
And the tears I've had to choke,
You've given me the will to fight,
With just a lick or stroke.
You seem to have the answer,
When I'm too screwed up to talk,
That wagging tail tells it all,
We'll just have to have a walk.
Love and life is so simple,
I seem to hear you say,
It's just releasing all your feelings,
To those that matter, come what may.
I've really learnt about myself,
In the time I've known you,
A dog is a man's best friend,
That's right, you know it's true.
But now, I ask myself,
What will I be without you?

Ron Wood

PETS' CORNER

As I recall when the children were young
In which animals played a big part
I can picture them all, in my mind's eye
For them, a special place in my heart.

First of all there was Tommy
The largest cat we ever saw,
Who lived till he was fourteen
Then we missed him more and more.

Hamsters, goldfish, stick insects,
Rabbits and guinea pigs too,
Try catching a hamster when he escapes
Can't count the times I've said 'Phew!'

Cheeky Charlie was a Chinese cock
Who pranced with spurs on his feet,
With six lovely hens to look after
Lived life to the full - so be it.

Snowy the bantam, who laid her eggs
In the back of our mini-van,
At eighteen years old, she was a beaut'
Record breakers, beat that if you can.

Then there was Pasha, an Irish setter
A wayward miss was she
Who presented us with ten lovely pups
A perfect mum to be.

Our children's lives were happy
Animals taught them how to care,
Being mindful of the needs of others
And knowing how to share.

Joyce White

WE DON'T HEAR THEM CRY

We are tampering with nature,
Which shouldn't be touched by mankind.
Killing innocent animals,
Just for vitamins and energy to keep us alive.

Nature is a precious thing,
Something that shouldn't be extinct.
Yet people go on experimenting,
No-one bothers to think.

Animals everywhere are suffering,
They have no choice to live or die.
Callous humans set out to kill them,
We don't hear them cry.

In butchers they are hanging,
Dripping in blood and fat.
Pain is all that animals have felt,
Doesn't seem like anyone cares about that.

I wonder what God really thinks,
About killing off his creations.
We all know what is happening
We don't need any explanations.

When you're licking your lips at dinner,
Just think about how it got there
The meat gets onto your plate,
Simply because some people just don't care.

Lee West

MY TWO FAITHFUL FRIENDS

My two cuddly friends
Are cuddly, loveable, also mischievous
Joy is like a princess
On a velvet cushion she loves to sit
Her huge wide eyes you cannot resist
By my side at bed time you will find her
She seems to understand my feelings
She knows when I'm lonely, even when I'm sick

The other one's called Snowy the cheekiest also nosy
When I'm in the bathtub
He sits watching every movement
I tell him he's just like any human
He's just like one of the boys
He sleeps at the other side of me
They are like two little soldiers guarding me

When we get up in the morning
Outside of the bathroom they wait
Then I say come on kids
And down the stairs we go
I try to get my breakfast
They look at me and seem to say
Please can we have ours first
So I just cannot resist my loveable pair
I'm sure no one could do you
Just two loveable cats, my friends are.

Evelyn Farr

THE CAGED LEOPARD

I am no part of your world - oh man,
older I am
than Egypt's ancient halls -
its vaulted temples
and its tombs of kings.

Still is my spirit the bearer of a seal
more ancient than the mystery
of the Sphinx;
lost to your world with the ashes
of time consumed -
you reduce me to a shadow on the ground.

Yet, do not ignore my soul - it is the fire
that burned before the sun
was god to pharaohs.
Then was my reign -
before the Earth was tamed
by the fierce and faltering cries
of human birth.

And so - oh man,
your cradle and your grave
are wise to shackle me
in measured space,
lest my escaping will might rearrange
the order
of my long neglected state!
For you and I -
fall keenly on our prey,
but unlike you -
I take no prisoners!

Sylvia Cole

BONNIE

How can I describe this horse we all loved,
She had beauty, she had grace, a lot of charm.
A wicked gleam in her eyes and a temper too,
But her love was repaid to all that she knew.

All the names she had been called,
And the threats have all been made.
When in the field she was at her best,
This is when your temper is put to the test.

Call her name and away she would go,
All around the field, but to you, oh no.
In the field you go with a bucket of food,
But all that you see is the air turning blue.

Through the air goes your wellington boot,
She looks at you and don't give a hoot.
At last your mind starts to think,
And from your pocket you take a Polo mint.

Now Bonnie's love for this mint is so strong,
She won't stay away from you very long.
Over she comes with a toss of her head,
The mint now gone, she can now be lead.

P B Ford

CAPTIVITY

The listless crowds move slowly past the cages
        in the stifling heat.
The child, a waving fern aloft for air,
        follows with dragging feet.

She shrinks towards her mother with a strangled cry -
        a chimpanzee
Is staring fixedly at her, his caged companions
        milling angrily.

142

He does not see the frightened child. The torrid air
    and waving frond
Have touched some chord. His eyes search anxiously
    for something far beyond . . .

Beneath a burning sky, the cool green freedom
    of the forest ways.
And in its mournful longing, infinitely sad
    his straining gaze.

Bertha Fox

DOG TRIALS

Showing dogs hubby does well
I can't show dogs it gives me hell
Can't trim either hubby does that too
All I seem to do is go out
And pick up poo
Clean dogs look after dogs
Puppies I rear well
Bathe dogs feed dogs
Never mind the smell
Early morning walks in
Ice and in the snow
Day after day it's all go
Rain hail fog sun
All in all it's supposed to be fun
Get ready for dog shows
A long long way away
Wake in the morning
To start another day

Patricia Flynn

WILDLIFE AT HEART
(For Ken Read 1926-1994. My Grandad)

A lonely grave sat all by itself
It wept in the shade
Cold and hurt
Colourful butterflies fluttered about the cool blue sky
Crickets jumped in the green grass
Frogs croaked on lilipads by watery ponds
Leaves ran from branches to bushes
Small children played joyfully in summer's heat
Foxes huddled up close to their young
Rabbits played merrily in straw fields
Boisterous laughter and friendly grins
Friends wrestle and fight in tattered uniforms
And Rambo like school ties were strung around our heads
Dirty shirts and muddy Nike trainers
Wishing flowers and bright buttercups
Swaying branches and running races
Scarecrows take rest to let crows perch on stiffened straw arms
And let summer's day end peacefully
Before having to walk home

Andrew Read

ANIMALS

Birds can fly
and honeybees too.
Fish can swim in rivers and sea.
The moon has come
and the sun has gone.
So it's time to see
the deep blue sea.

Suzanne Rickard (7)

WOMAN'S BEST FRIEND

Oh what a posh house this would be
Without your muddy paws,
The postman's fingers all intact
Without your snapping jaws.

My duvet would lie undisturbed
Not in a crumpled mass,
No ghastly trophies you've thrown up
After devouring grass.

No freezing tramps through wind and rain,
I'd curl up by the fire,
No dog hairs on the Axminster
The hoover could retire.

White pristine paintwork, not a scratch
Would mar its satin sheen,
No smudges on the window panes
Where your wet nose had been.

Full unmolested rubbish bags
Could hover by the gate,
Bin-men could call unterrorised
Without you there in wait.

Plants in the garden would survive,
Flowers blooming all about,
No lethal earthy trenches where
You'd tried to tunnel out.

But on my blackest days when I'm
Shunned by the human race,
Life would be quite unbearable
Without your loving face.

Jenni J Moores

MY ANIMALS

My little dog Midge, my faithful friend,
Scruffy, affectionate, and loyal companion,
No yard long pedigree, just a mixture,
Mum was a poodle, Dad was a terrier,
Midge is good with children, and likes to play
With my grandchildren, when they stay for a day.
She loves her walks, is obedient on the road,
A good house dog, and barks if anyone is around,
If I go out shopping, and leave her alone,
Midge is so pleased to see me, when I get home.

There is also Gem, my brown stripey cat,
Getting older, and sleeps a lot.
Spends most of her time around the house
In warmer weather, curls up in the greenhouse
Gem and Midge get on well, they are good friends
And at times, chase each other around the garden,
But if a strange cat comes inside our gate,
Midge barks like mad, and the cat soon escapes.
When it's cold and wet, they both sleep by the fire
They are good company for me, now I have retired.

Lorna June Burdon

LOST - A BLACK CAT

Old Meg puts her hands down gently,
As she sits in her fireside chair,
She moves them ever so gently,
To search for silken black hair.

Old Meg puts her hands down gently,
As she comes to the end of each day.
Is she lost? Is she hurt? Is she hiding?
Who has taken her Blackie away?

Peter Donaldson

TRUST

'My' wild blackbird - at my call - would fly down and stay
Nigh - showing trust - almost as a child may;
Alas, through time - he has had his day.
'Our' families of sparrows, and others - each day -
Feed and bathe - 'at home' - and fly not far away.

In the wild - a timid deer - soft eyed creature -
The colour of its coat will blend with nature;
A way it can defend - by motionless feature -
And, if, for food, it must depend -
Trust in man may come, and fear not deter.

In the home - a puppy - a canine 'child' who plays!
Bright-eyed and questioning - trust conveys
For its well being - with love, faithfully repays.
A kitten - so much for it to discover -
The house is such an adventurous place!
Outside, under the watchful eye of its mother -
The garden - full of wonderful things to chase!

Mildred E Wood

CANINE FRIEND

He stands by my side
waiting to guide
me to pastures new,
he sees through my eyes
the same sunrise
faithful he is and wise.
When I am old
and life gets cold
he charms his way
into my soul.

Joan Isabel Hands

NICE WEATHER

A sharp updraft strikes my face
Clouds pile up like crashed traffic
Flees twilight as I foully trudge
Khaki Campbell ducks to shed.

Hush on the water for the god of thunder
As his hammer greets the anvil heads
The downpour begins as lightning glimmers
The pond ripples alive with wings
Beating the rhythm rejoicing ducks.
Beaks are mining the bank to enlarge
The realm ruled by webbed feet
Plumage washed, nurtured livery
Transversing the water diving for dinner.
The rain games at ducks and drakes
Their musical chatter blends with rumbles.

How can I be happy in storms
Skin soaked, thoughts chilled?
Ducks' enjoyment resounds deep
I realise my body is dancing with the rain.

Martin Vine

IN MEMORY OF PETER

I will always remember my best friend
He never failed a helping paw to lend
In times of sadness he was always there
A kiss and a lick to show he cared.

His name was Peter my loyal canine friend
A friend like no other was he to me
Never asking questions as trusting as could be
Trusting me to feed him and his coat to tend.

We would go out walking in a country lane
Never would he stray from my side until we were home again.
Then as the years rolled by he became very lame
Vet said he could not help. He would always be the same.

Early one morning our postman left the gate ajar.
My best friend wondered out, he could not have gone far.
I heard a mournful whimper it was Peter he did look very grim.
Some cruel person had shot him. He will never
                    be dead to me for I love him so.

I Barton

MY TRUE FRIEND

A beautiful coat, a long wagging tail,
Two trusting brown eyes, set never to fail,
A temperament that is second to none,
A bark not to threaten, but just to have fun,
A nature so loving, and loyal, and true,
She'll stay right beside you whatever you do,
If you're down or upset with her head on your knee
Her look says you can always depend upon me,
Just play with my toys, or a stroke or a cuddle,
Then be more like me for life's not such a struggle,
For all that I need is to play, or a walk,
For dinner I don't need a knife or a fork,
Don't worry if mud's on the floor, over there,
It's me that lies on it, for you've got a chair,
If you were like me you could sleep all the day,
And never worry about wages or pay,
I don't need any money, or a door with a key,
I just need your love, and that comes for free.

Sandy Fryer

WHY?

My friends are of the feline kind
Both gracious and at times refined
But there are questions I would like to ask
Mysteries I would like unmasked

Why, for instance when I'm asleep
Must you in silence wish to creep
Then on my pillow sit and talk
And all my movements must you stalk?

So I'm awake at the crack of dawn
And as I watch you begin to yawn
Then I catch sight of the gift you brought
An unfortunate mouse that you have caught

You then choose, on warm sunny days
A spot to sprawl and then to laze
But why my friends must it be so
That it's where my favourite flowers grow?

And sometimes when I call your name
It seems to be your favourite game
To sit quite motionless and stare
And look at me without a care

And why is it when I try to read
You seem to feel the constant need
To have to take up centre stage
By sitting on the middle page

With all these answers still to find
I think what I should bear in mind
One plain and very simple fact
Is that my friend you are a cat.

Paula Stedman

THE PAW THAT DIGS THE GROUND RULES THE GARDEN

Mr Ross of Chestwood Lodge was a dapper dog when young,
With shining coat, bib and socks and tail that was well hung.
Through the years that have gone by he'd help and supervise,
On how the garden should be dug and how the flowers should rise.

Mr Ross's special place was by the washing pole
Where a collection of stones and sticks piled up beside a hole,
And as the sun warmed up on sunny summer days
You'd find him sleeping by his pile and that's where he would stay.

Time turns the page on my dear friend his back legs all arey
Brown eyes clouded now with age it's almost his goodbye.
There's a spot beside the tree where blossoms fall in spring,
And forever he will rest 'neath daisies' pretty ring.

Sally Crook-Ford

MOLLY - A MUCH LOVED CAT

I watch her from my cottage doorway
On the first morning of spring
Lying, in total indolence
Under the hedge of blackthorn blossom
Bathing in the sunshine
At peace with the world
No worries, no fears
Just pure pleasure in being alive
Secure and safe in a comfy spot
She has known for years
Confident in the knowledge of her superiority
Indifferent to my adoration
Speckled with blackthorn petals
Stretched out motionless
Enjoying the early morning sun.

Pamela Kercher

KITTY THE CAT

This is a story of a cat,
Kitty is her name,
she's not real, she's make believe,
you'll like it just the same,

Kitty the cat,
had a lovely home,
all day long,
she would roam

when she was tired,
she'd take a nap,
curled up in,
her owner's lap,

she was a really happy cat,
she rarely ever got wrong,
she'd sit upon the window sill,
singing a little song,

every trick that Kitty played,
gave everyone lots of pleasure,
and everyone considered her,
as their little treasure,

Kitty was a lovely cat,
she loved lying in the sun,
she played with all the children,
they really had some fun,

the children all loved Kitty,
she had always been their friend,
and she always would be,
until the very end.

Christine Wright

THE SECRET OF THE ELEPHANT

They say an elephant never forgets
My elephant never forgets
To keep and share my precious secret
To guard me through the night
To make everything alright

One charming unguarded moment
From many moments, months and years
Of unrealism and fears
My elephant only hears
And never forgets

Elephant you are true to me
You are always there
So I forget to care
Instead I am spellbound
Without the sound
I just turn around
                    to you
And I know what to do

I dream of the one unguarded moment
The precious memory
So I just keep living and giving

You look like you're made of clay
But we know every day
You *are* real
To steal - my mind
For a while - to dream
To keep and share my precious secret
I don't forget
My elephant never forgets

Peggy Ruth Banks

REINCARNATION (MANY HAPPY RETURNS)

I shot an old buck rabbit by the churchyard wall today
And that old buck was nibbling grass on my friend Miley's grave
And then I got to thinking that when I eat yon old buck
A part of me will be a part of him the good Lord took

And then I got to thinking about Farmer Snowden's sheep
They graze all round them tombstones where the village fathers sleep
And everyone int' village likes some mutton now and then
So part of everyone int' graves must be a part of them

But then I got to thinking about them as went upt' stack
Surely there was no way none of them was coming back
Or was cremation not the end? - Perhaps there was a sequel
Maybe it's not just cats and dogs - maybe it's raining people

Although my mates have gone away upt' crematorium chimney
Their vapours come back down int' rain and onto fields of barley
I cannot sup a glass with friends that's left this earthly vale
But in a funny kind of way they still provides my ale

So then I got to thinking; no one really stays below
They only gets recycled - comes back for another go
And this must have been going on since living things first started
So everyone int' world is really them as has departed.

Thomas J Pink

FOR LIFE

Each animal which comes into our care
we should look after.
But do we?
Some are dumped, some are so cruelly treated, that it
brings tears to our eyes.
We should ask ourselves why,
But do we?
Animals are something for life not for a week or a
month
They give their love to us for keeps.
Trust us with their lives to be looked after.
They don't ask for us to take them in we chose ourselves,
and it is up to us to make sure we will look after them
for the rest of their
life.

Dee Lean

A HORSE CALLED FANCY

Fancy was beautiful, she stood out in a crowd.
Lovely, my granddaughter said, to jump and to ride.
When she jumped in the shows, the applause was loud.
The many rosettes that she won are displayed with pride.
The two moving together, were like poetry in motion.
Fancy was treasured, and looked after with care and devotion.
Her life was happy and free,
Until one day it ended when she fell.
Her leg was broken and the vet couldn't save her.
They buried her in a corner of the field, under a tree.
In the fullness of time her stable companion Harriet had a foal.
She chose to have her baby under that very same tree,
What else would we call her, but Fancy free.

Olive Partridge

SHEP

He lies in peace
In our garden at rest
Our beloved Shep
Was one of the best,
The flowers I plant
Are for him alone
How much we miss him
No one will ever know,
The memories of him
And the joy he gave
I will always remember
For the rest of my days,
A loving friend
A good companion too
No other dog was quite like you,
I never thought I'd cry so much
When our dear Shep
Was taken from us.

Elizabeth Hoggett

MY CAT

Emerald green eyes,
pink tipped nose;
furry body,
padded toes.

In this house,
she reigns supreme;
I the servant,
she the queen.

Pearl Surman

PRIZEWINNER

There are dreams reflected
In your rich, brown eyes
Of bracken and the woods at dawn,
As you paw my palm,
Dog-like,
Pink tongue a-loll.
What a pity, Donovan,
That you cannot understand
A word of what I say;
But then, perhaps -
Perhaps there's more to you,
More than I previously knew;
Maybe you see the past
In my mind's mirrors,
My weaknesses - regrets -
And, yes, loves too;
Perhaps there's even more
To you
Than what they said at Crufts;
I wonder -
Well-groomed, yes,
You're that and more -
A thoroughbred -
From head to tail,
Alert, intelligent and lithe -
The lot -
But the soul's secrets
Lie just between us two.

Ruth Daviat

MY HORSE

Come on, come on, ride with all your might.
Go fast, speed of light.
Excitement! Longed for this day
My horse actually came all this way.

First glimpse trotting in a field.
Brown shiny coat, stood fourteen hands
tall.
Well groomed, 'thought', do well.

Saw potential.
Said, 'She's for me.'
Welcome Carrie Mulahon, learn to swiftly run.

Brought in experts.
Worked together until you were tops.
Time arrived, girl. 'Ascot'.
I proudly stand, can't believe what I see.
Run run you heard me,
Answered, 'Neigh.'

Front of my eyes, nose ahead.
Won three thirty race.
'Gold stakes'.
Ran up side of course, placed blanket coat.
Few extra lumps sugar, treat.
Holding reins led past grandstand seats.
To sound happy cheering punters, who had bet
Money on.
'Carrie Mulahon'.

Dawn Constable

THE WHITE DOE OF SANDIA PEAK

On a sheer, cold ridge, soaring above the desert plain
We rested, feeling again the scant warmth
Of hazy sun upon our weathered faces.
A lazy tiredness sighed through our complaining limbs
And we floated wantonly into soft, delicious sleep.
Awakened by the creep of long, shivering shadows,
I saw my companion lying alone in a mist of dreams.
I roused him and we readied for our descent;
Down through streams of ice, over crystal slopes,
Tinted by the winter sun, a glowing peach.
We reached the snow-trodden track of our ascent
And traversed through dense white wood.

My comrade spoke and I heard the crack of a twig
As it broke beneath the rumble of startled feet.
Then, among pale stems of naked aspen, we saw her,
A lone white doe, melding into snow-covered banks.
I caught her restive gaze. I saw her breath, her fear.
I wanted to caress those smooth white flanks,
I whispered, 'Don't be afraid, let me draw near.'
She stared at me, nervously poised, ready to run.
'I won't hurt you. I just want to touch you!'
But she was off, leaping through silver beams of sun.
We silently watched her go, and slowly resumed
Our lonely descent, through deep and leaden snow.

John Merritt

THE CHRISTENING OF CHLOÉ

I christened my cat on Sunday
She is gently loving and kind
I made a cross upon her head
And prayed that she could find
The love of God protecting her
When to roam she had a mind
I thanked God for the love she shows
A companion kind and sincere
She knows my every mood and move
And I love to have her near
She sleeps upon my bed at night
She knows I am alone
Paws my face with a gentle touch
If she wants to leave the room
She is really concerned if I am not feeling well .
Has a worried look and tries to tell
That she cares for me and all is well
She is pure white with pink nose and ears
A very special cat
Christened and blessed with the love of God
A truly Holy cat
She is my best and special friend
Apart from God above.
If she leaves this earthly plane before me,
She will wait with patience and love.
She is one of God's creatures.
And I know that we shall
Meet again in His Heaven above.

Evelyn A Evans

THE BROWN BULL

There he stands, all alone,
Far from the herd.
It's half- past three, I think
He's looking for me.
I remember the day he was born,
He was so small, and now we're both
so tall.

We had to sell up, once Dad passed on,
The farm was too big and the debts
got us all.
Mr Clark runs it now, and makes a
good job.

I'm the school master, running the school,
Leaving, at the end of the day
I think of old Ned,
He's waiting for me,
So I take the old road, up to the farm.

Marie Dorrian

UNTITLED

Our tortoise Joe is very old,
And must not hibernate I'm told,
When winter comes, he likes to stay
By the side of the Aga every day
Waking each morn, for his favourite sweet corn.

Stretched out in her basket, our little cat Fleur,
Likes him for a footrest, he makes her purr.
How peaceful to watch them sharing together
Warmth and love, with no care for the weather.

Eva Savage

DOLPHIN, MY DEAREST DOLPHIN

No! Don't hurt the dolphins, their home, is in the sea,
not only that, I was drowning once and one rescued me.
It carried me ashore, must have caught sight of me,
before I hit the ocean floor.

Please, don't hurt the dolphins who's home is in the sea.
They would not hurt you, whether they be many, or,
whether they be few.
Who knows, perhaps if you were drowning, this fishy
friend would rescue, you!

He was singing me a song as he carried me along.
His words were not clear because my little heart was,
full of fear.
I did not want to drown, did not want to wear the
ocean, as a permanent dressing gown.

He tossed me onto the land, if he were human,
I'd have held his hand, kissed his cheek,
for saving me, from the depth of the sea!
I saw many things, yes, more than a peek,
now I know, some things we should never seek!

So please, leave them alone, their home is in the ocean,
with its waves so wild and free.
I'll never forget the one that rescued me,
before I hit the bottom of the sea,
maybe, that dolphin was watching me.

Alison McGinty

162

FURRY FRIENDS

Do you like furry friends?
We do, dogs and cats.
We have a kitten
She curls around your feet
She gets upon your lap
Then you hear a little knock
Then a little tap.

'Where's fluffy gone?
'Oh, she's off out,
Through the cat flap.'

She's down the garden,
She's getting ready to pounce,
She's after the birds,
Or is it the mice,
Oh no, I can't look,
I shut my eyes,
Then open them.
She's coming home
With something in her mouth.
I'll shout
I'll cause a din
Because her dinner
Comes out of a tin.

Patricia B

FOUR RED ELEPHANTS

Here stand four red elephants,
carved in all their glory,
with curves so fine to show their strength,
the four red elephants stand proud.

They are the symbol of greatness,
as they move along the wasted land,
like huge carved rocks being guided by the wind,
they know where they stand.

As they listen for the voice of the river,
they hear only the un-natural voice of man's great knowledge,
these sculptured figures move swiftly with all their might,
but, they fear they will lose their fight.

The voices of man echo near,
with thoughts of only his greed,
for this is what man has come to respect,
is there really any need?

Here lay four red elephants,
carved in all their glory,
with curves so fine to show their strength,
our four red elephants lay proud.

Maria Backo

BEST FRIENDS

I love my Dad - he's my best mate
All others I find second rate.
I'm always with him at his side
And in the car with him I'll ride.
I had a most unhappy start
My mum and I were bound to part,
But then I went to live somewhere
With people who just didn't care.
The next place was a home for strays,
Then out for just a couple of days,
Next thing I'm back inside the home,
With not much space to freely roam.
And then two people came to see
And I thought he's the one for me.
I stood and hoped I looked my best
And wondered, have I passed the Test?

N J Whitehouse

GONE AWAY

A dish unwashed upon the kitchen floor,
old foot prints beside the door
that bit of biscuit found beneath the sink,
a ball, a rubber toy, a lead,
an empty bowl, once full, to drink.
No bark when the front bell rings.
No greeting leap, among other things.
That space to fill, that's all around,
the hollow emptiness of sound.
Unashamed tears fall upon this page.
He's gone; and what is left is inner rage.

Tom Gull

THE NIGHT TIME VISITOR

Laying in my tent in the dark of the night,
I try not to move with all my might.
I feel something creeping on the outside,
I felt so scared I could have cried.

Then it went quiet and the noises all stopped,
I listened for a while, then into a sleep I then dropped.
The next night we waited to see if they came back,
What ever it was it had removed a rubbish sack.

As midnight approached I heard a branch break,
It then shook my nerves until I was wide awake.
Then it appeared right out of the dark,
It was a vixen that had made its mark.

It was a beautiful colour with a bushy tail
After hours of waiting I knew we wouldn't fail.
Around the camp fire it walked, eating all that it could,
Watching this wild creature it made me feel so good.

It crept around the camp so sleek and so sly,
The quick little vixen , it seemed so shy.
She went over the field so she could fetch her mate,
So while they were gone, I put some food out on a plate.

We stayed in our tent and we waited a little while,
And as they came back, I couldn't help but smile.
I am sure they knew we were watching while they are their meal,
Because when they were finished, they both took to their heel.

That night will be remembered for the rest of my life,
The time I saw the wild fox and his lovely wife.
These memories I have, will always be filed,
Always remembering those foxes out in the wild.

Angie Armstrong

166

LITTLE FRIEND PEBBLES

So alive full of fun
A great joy in my life
Early morn till day is done
You brighten time like the morning sun
Two little eyes that shine
Look at me with adoration
A meow, meow cries it's time
So full of contemplation
White furry coat pink nose
Pretty as a picture
A lump in the throat grows
One look just says
As you endear yourself to those
Who admire your name Pebbles
Happy days we spend together
You know my every word
So playful and clever
Long may we understand
When you purr purr purr

Janet L Murray

GOODBYE MY FRIEND

I love you, was the last thing I said
I love you, I whispered as I kissed your head
The time had come to say goodbye
But the thought of losing you just made me cry
You slowly drifted away from me
The tears in my eyes made it hard to see
I sat and cradled you in my arms
And recited one of the holy psalms
Then I said a prayer to God
Please take care of my friend, my dog!

Colleen Knight

REQUIEM FOR A STRAY CAT

He walked into the house and made himself at home.
With not a shadow of a doubt. He walked right in
Eyes full of hope and trust, and tail held high,
Hoping to find a place to spend the night in.

Could I reject such trust, and turn my back on him,
Denying him shelter he was seeking?
Turning my back on him, turn him away,
Not listening to the words those eyes were speaking?

Such joy he brought me in the years that followed.
In sickness, and in health, he saw me through
With throaty purrings, snuggling up to me,
Giving his love the only way he knew.

And so the years went by, and he grew old with me.
His days of hunting birds and mice were put aside
For days of sleeping in the sun, or snoozing by the fire
Until, one day in summer, sadly he died.

If there's a Pussy-Heaven - surely there must be -
He's there among the angels, chasing voles.
He'll never harm them, even should he catch one,
For he and they are all immortal souls.

Be happy in your heaven, little fellow,
Where little Pussy-Angels have no pain.
I miss you now you've gone, the house feels empty,
- But you'll never need to see the vet again.

E M Summers

THE BENGAL TIGER

Bengal tiger, nocturnal and solitary,
Deters intruders, mark their territory.
Markings of gold, black and red,
Stands out when seen in the zoo.
But deep in forest or reed bed,
Stripes enable him to disappear from view.
They dislike excessive heat.
Often laze in water deep and cool.
Quench thirst at nearest stream or pool.
Driven by its need for meat,
Hunts down prey, wild boar and deer.
Attacks from the side or rear,
Capable of killing animals twice its size,
One of nature's most feared predators alive.
Evokes in man fear and awe.
Catches prey in its powerful jaw.
This fierce animal lives in Bengal,
Also in Burma and Nepal,
This beast is strictly carnivore,
Males can weigh 250KG or more.

K Brown

FIVE DONKEYS IN THE MEWS

I still remember the feeling, the day I read the news
It sent my senses reeling, what happened in the mews.
The slaughter of five donkeys in the middle of the night,
my imagination working overtime on the gruesome, bloody sight.
The senseless, mindless morons, with slashing, sharpened knives,
stole upon the innocent beasts and took from them their lives.
If, for just one moment, they could take the place
Of one defenceless creature and how it feels to face,
the terror which is deemed at will, the bloody butchers
with their futile kill.

Sandi Isaac

MISTY

She was eleven weeks old, when I bought her.
And as white, as the pure driven snow.
She had a face, with a beauty that would haunt you.
And a love, that we were privileged to know.

Earlier in life, one of our children
Had been alarmed, by a dog that had strayed.
And so by bringing Misty, into their life.
This was going to be the answer I prayed.

My wife stated 'I'm not an animal lover!
But when Misty appeared out of the cold
Her dislike, turned to love and affection
An emotion, that was returned a thousand fold.

I need never have held any, reservations
For all the joys and happiness, she brought.
Our home was filled with love, for each other.
And now, a special love that she taught.

Her temperament, was one of an angel.
Her mannerism, you could take her anywhere.
She was never selfish, or demanding.
And for all of us, she would always be there.

She not only brought us companionship.
She didn't only bring us love.
She brought to us, a greater understanding.
Of a different life, from God up above.

Now she's gone, she will never be forgotten.
In our thoughts, she will always be there
When a part of your life, has sadly left you.
There will always be a vacant chair.

T I Graham

CALLING ALL ANIMAL LOVERS

Have you seen that adorable
Cute pup,
With the brown eyes?
Well it's in the shelter
now
Well it very nearly
died.

Calling all animal lovers
I ask you to show that
you care
Give money to this
charity
So animals have food
and shelter to share

The pup arrived bruised
and battered
its owner didn't care
and was cruel

Each and every animal
can become a friend
Let us all be generous
and kind

Animals are the best friends
we will ever find.

With shelter all the animals
have a home
they really need the money
to give the pets security
calling all animal lovers
Make them your sisters and brothers.

Jody Baxter

LADY AND TRAMP

You'll probably say 'She was just a pet'
But to us she was the most special yet
A trusted companion she also became
Friendly by nature and very tame

Her vigilant interests came into their own
When the turkey was placed in the laundry room
Guarding all day with the cats in full flight
How was she to know that the door was shut tight?

The settee was her target as evening drew near
Lying in wait with her long floppy ears
Listening for footsteps to tell her when
The time had come for a cuddle again

She was so observant and knew every move
Which made us feel guilty when we donned our shoes
She would look so pathetic with those large brown eyes
And seemed to be saying 'I don't like goodbyes'

But dear little Lady has now lost her zest
For without *goodbye* she found peace and rest
Her close friend Tramp has pined for a while
But with love and affection he now shows a smile

Though just a plodder, with one ear cocked
His rough coat wiry and tummy well stocked
He's so inoffensive and happy to be
A cute loving member of our family

This little chap has such gentle ways
And who could resist his appealing gaze?
'I might not be glamorous' he's trying to say
'But thank you for loving me day by day'

Grace Mary Neary

PUPPY'S THOUGHTS

Please, give a thought,
before I'm bought.
For I'm only a puppy and,
I'll have to be taught.

I'm vulnerable you see,
So, responsible you'll have to be.
For instance I'll need a nice clean
bed to rest my tiny head,
Oh! And not forgetting I'll
have to be fed.

Daily a walk would be nice,
preferably once or twice.
When you're away, at home
I'll stay, which is no fun,
when all you walk to do is play.

I wish I could talk but, I
can't only walk.
So, remember my plea,
for you have to see that
I have feelings too and if
you have not then please,
don't buy me.

Sandra Almond

173

A DOG'S LIFE!

I may be a mongrel
But I still have my dreams
I'm ducking and diving
And weaving my schemes

If I won a fortune
Then I would have fame
I may win your heart
And you'd take my name

Then I would be Solomon
Your *pal* and your *chum*
You'd be my *Sheba*
My queen and a mum.

No longer a mongrel
A *pedigree* sire
Living the high life
And we could retire.

To *win a lot*
Is my dearest wish
We could eat caviar
And expensive fish

I'd buy you a salmon
Champagne and fresh cream . . .
If I won the lottery

But it's only a dream!

Stephen Friede

MOST DEFINITELY MAN'S BEST FRIEND!

When considering to buy a family pet
There are many things that you mustn't forget.
The size of your house, the price of the food,
Also observe the breed's temperamental mood!

If you live on a farm and you need a go-getter,
Then look no further than an Irish red setter,
And if you need help to look after your stock,
Then a collie can sort our your wandering flock.

If it is your house that you want to protect,
Then a doberman pincher is the one to select.
Although some people simply don't have the room
So a jack russell would do the same job, I presume.

If you need a dog to help guide the blind,
Then a labrador is the best you will find.
The policeman's favourite is the good old alsation
Who'll always be welcome down at the station.

The aforementioned dogs are all pedigree
Which all of us recognise as soon as we see.
But interbreeding can cause lots of upsets,
So they can cost you a fortune down at the vets.

Most people just want a canine companion
A puppy that they can truly depend on,
And what better type than one of mixed breed
Who will fetch your slippers, and a paper to read!

Sally Boast

WONDERFUL DYLAN -OUR OLD ENGLISH SHEEPDOG

Lovely, hairy, four feet by two,
Blue-eyed with it, gentle too,
Good natured, white and grey,
He brings you things as if to say,

Play with me do not muck about,
Throw me things but do not shout!
He's always a welcome at the door,
He finds no-one a dreadful bore.

To and fro he loves to carry,
For his master Barry.
Every morning and end of day,
He loves to go walkies and to stray,

Race and chase a football in the dark,
To him it's all a lovely lark.
He is a member of the house,
He takes his orders without a grouse.

He is ever so very willing,
He's a dog? Well he's our Dylan.

Percy J Rowat

STAR AND I

Never a partnership did you see
Than my feisty star and me
With a toss of her head and a swish of her tail
We're off! Galloping through moor and dale

She flies like the wind on a restless night
And I'd swear on occasions she'd even take flight
Heart and hoof beating as one
With both our heads turned up to the sun

The splash of the water as she crosses a stream
Such freedom could never be caught in a dream
When we are apart it's never the same
But together we ride for the love of the game

The glory of winning was not in our plan
But to reach out and take life with both hands if we can
Like a streak of lightning across the sky
That's how it is with star and I

Amanda Everatt

RAIDERS!

'Psst, come on Lucy, the coast is clear,' Amy calls out to her twin,
'Come over here to the cupboard, it's easy to break in!'
Amy stretches up her paw, for opening doors she's got the knack,
Lucy watches and sighs enviously 'Oh how I wish I could do that.'
'Come on Lucy, get right in there's room enough for two,
Just take a look around you, there's stacks and stacks of food!'
'But this is mainly dog food - still it smells good just the same.'
Replies Amy 'If we eat the dog food, the dog'll take the blame!'
They munched away the pair of them, so engrossed they didn't hear,
The sound of human footsteps coming down the stairs,
Into the kitchen their owner came, looking for her cats,
She saw the cupboard door ajar - she'd caught them in the act!
Lucy backed out hastily and Amy followed suit,
They both sat looking charming, innocent and cute,
But their owner knew the truth for there were crumbs upon the floor,
'To make this cupboard cat-proof it'll need a lock put on the door.'
Lucy and Amy slipped away while their owner cleared up the mess,
'You know,' said Lucy, 'I'm not quite sure, but I think perhaps she guessed!'

Cathy Houghton

MY FRIEND

My friend,
To you I owe
My life.
I feel your warmth,
Forever there,
By my side;
Strong and obedient.
I depend on you.
A friendship based
On trust -
A marriage.
Always forgiving,
Always loyal,
Never distracted.
We grow together,
United
In our love.
I promise
To be there for you
Always.
And hope you will be too,
For without you
I am blind.

Jane H Skoulding

ORIENTAL

Nomis, Nomis, a brighter
                  shade of white,
Sees with his fine eyes
The darkness of the night.
Purrs and thinks
Thinks and purrs
Of his quiet delights
Nomis, Nomis a brighter
                  shade of white.
Say his name backwards
Sing it once again . . .
For he is a handsome cat
As he hunts in the lane.
Nomis, Nomis a brighter shade of white,
Twitches his long whiskers
As he snugly sits tight!

L Brown

ODE TO A DEPARTED PET

My white poodle Petra
Was always extra
Special to me
As together we
Walked in the country
Where she could run free
Have fun rabbit chasing
Or dead twigs replacing
With a turn roundabout
And her tongue hanging out
She'd run to my side
Laughing eyes open wide
As if to say
What a wonderful day

Yvonne V Smith

OLD SADIE

I sit alone and wait by the garden gate.
I know you're out, but should not be late,
With my head and feet I open the door,
But the gate need more than a paw.
There's a gap in the hedge but I'm too big.
I might get out if I start to dig.
So I decide to turn on my charm.
I'd hate it if you came to any harm.
When I was a pup, you were a grown lad.
The only pal I truly had.
But you have grown into a man.
And takes me out whenever you can.
Across the fields you let me run.
Having a game with you is still fun.
But I wonder how long it will be.
When you realise I can hardly see.
Every time I'm ill you fetch the vet.
But I've noticed you have not yet.
Well master I am getting slow and old
7 years to 1 so I've been often told
Well I could go off in my sleep
And my memories I know you'll keep.

Margaret Upson

OUR LITTLE DEAF WHITE CAT

At last the eagerly awaited day had come
Our chosen kitten was now old enough to leave his mum
My husband eagerly rushed home bearing a ball of white fluff
You captured our hearts with your eyes of blue, one look was enough

But within a day or two one sad thing had become clear
Your little ears could not one single thing hear.
But already your cute little ways had won my heart
We couldn't take you back, with you we couldn't bear to part.

But there was a plus side to your infirmity
Not hearing all the harsh sounds of life gave you serenity.
You could never hear a cross or angry voice
Everyone to you was a potential new friend in whom to rejoice

One day at the window I doubled up with laughter
A large alsation ran from the garden with you running after
As he ran, bewildered, tail between his legs, broken down
He couldn't understand why when he barked so fiercely your look
said, 'You clown!'

Every open cupboard was an invitation for you to rush inside
Every cardboard box brought into the house, a place for you to hide
Into everything we did you poked your nose so pink and small
You were determined not to be left out of anything at all

If I tried to entice you from the step full of disdain was your look
But when you wanted to lie on my lap you just trampled paper or book
As I chatted to you, in my arms, my husband gave me a look so grim
'I'm listening to the TV, just move your lips, it's all the same to him.

After many years you began to tire, your movements slow,
Then one morning you laid down and died in the early morning glow
You were called Bianco, because as the advert said,
You were the white one, the right one, now sadly dead.

Margaret Meagher

CANINE PET

Our dog knows he's the boss,
And thinks I'm his fool, to cross,
He's black and tan, he thinks he's man,
He reads in bed, my spouse said,
He takes newspapers out the rack,
When we're in bed,
We know when someone's about,
For he barks and barks until we shout,
It doesn't matter if the next door neighbours,
Are coming in, he kicks up a din,
For he thinks he owns us, neighbours,
Street, an' all,
He can't stand birds and cats, alike,
If they're in our garden he wants a fight,
And he's first in bed at night,
He can't put up with us out of sight,
I have to laugh though when I hear my spouse moan
They're my slippers, get your own,
When we take him walkies over the park,
He'll pinch a football from some bright spark,
He thinks he's a footballer, or a referee's nark,
Trying taking it off him and he'll just bark and bark,
But I wouldn't change him, my canine pet,
I think I'd grieve myself to death.

Joan McAvoy

EVERY HOME SHOULD HAVE ONE (OR TWO)

What a sad day when our dear cat died,
Without Tigger there was a large gap;
We missed the feel of fur round our legs,
And the friendly noise of his door flap.

Tigger will never be forgotten,
But a cat-less home wears a sad face,
So quite soon we went to the cats' home
To find another to take his place.

Two little waifs clinging together,
Looking so frightened and very small,
Once owned by gypsies who tired of them,
Unwanted, hurled them over a wall.

Shivering with fear and painfully thin,
The gypsies had left them to their fate,
There was no choice, we had to have both!
Our hearts were touched by their sorry state.

At first they weren't like kittens should be,
We had to help them both learn to play.
They shrank from touch and jumped at all noise,
And hid under the dresser all day.

But with patient love they settled in,
Their little tummies with food grew round,
They began to like sitting on laps,
Their first purr was a wonderful sound!

We feel so blessed with our little cats,
And delight in the mutual rapport,
Animals, like us, respond to love,
And in return give us so much more.

Mary Care

THEY NEVER FORGET

I've heard that pets have short memories, can you really believe that!
Our dogs know lots and remember what's what, and for intelligence
                                                    talk to our cat.
Remembering things he even sings, Rover certainly has brains you can tell
Sooty's quick and is slick and at dinner-time even rings his own little bell.

They remember the time, you don't have to mime, each movement
                                        you make is a sign . . .
. . . that it's time to get up, they're hungry to sup and even know when
                                        it's their bedtime
With ways they do reach, just lacking in speech, really they're like one of us
If some of our friends could make such amends, man's best friend
                                        gives him so much more fuss

The love in their eyes will never surprise, they're so faithful, graceful
                                        and loved
But to say *can't remember*, when from Jan' to December, they will
be close like a hand that's well gloved.

Lucy May Bloxham

ANIMAL THOUGHT

If I was an animal
I would dread the rain;
Dread the drought,
Fear the bondage and the whip
And life outdoors, in winter's icy grip.

I would fear the hunter,
Those who stole my land;
Wishing for sanctuary
And a kind and gentle hand.

184

I would hope I didn't know,
About becoming old and worn;
When nobody would want me,
Past my best, not worth my corn.

I would hope for someone kind,
To come and care for me;
To let me share this world
And live with dignity.

Pauline Boncey

FRIEND OF A FRIEND

I have a friend who's acquired a cat
(Personally, I'm not all that
compatible with felines)
It chose her, not she it
But now there's mutual benefit
Apparently it made a beeline
To her door
And stayed
It's bony, white, aristocratic
Enigmatic
No doubt who's boss around the place
Sits regally on a cupboard top
I cringe, expecting him to drop
On me
(I think he's on my case!)
My friend is willing slave to it
to wit -
They rub along together
He has found a comfy pad
She has grown to love the lad
Chums, I think, forever
On Cat's terms however!

Jo Lee

GISMO

My name is Gismo
And life's been rather sad
As a puppy taken from my mum
And treated very bad

At first they seemed to like me
They bought me lots of toys
I felt very happy
Contented full of joy

I soon found I was very wrong
Some days I had no meat
I was very undernourished
And had sores upon my feet

I was taken to a kennel
Cleaned up and given food
I was feeling very lonely
But they treated me real good

Alone I sat within my pen
Feeling sad and glum
A lady simply stopped and stared
Could she be my new mum

Some people came and bought me
They took me to their home
At first I was frightened
And awfully alone

My life is very happy now
I'm having lots of fun
There's a lovely garden here
Where I can go and run

Gillian Morrisey

FOXY-LADY

They didn't want her - anymore; they could ignore the upheld paw.
They wouldn't see the wagging tail, beating tattoos, on the stair rail.
They didn't want her anymore, they watched her walk out of the door.
They never even said, 'Goodbye,' to the little dog, twelve inches high!

They didn't want her adoring love, they threw her out, like a worn out glove!
They used her, cruelly, like a battery hen, kept her caged - in a small, wooden pen.
Poor Foxy-Lady, as was her name, decided she must be to blame.
They didn't want her - anymore; her little doggy heart, was sore.

This little Cairn, filled with fright, was such a sad, heart-rending sight.
With matted fur and teeth knocked out, human kindness - in so much doubt!
They didn't want her - anymore. But, someone did, who knew the score.
They took this dog, twelve inches high, gave her soft cushions on which to lie.

They fed her, brushed her tangled coat and to the vet, they did her tote.
They gently calmed her frightened shakes, and showed her, quickly, what kindness makes.
A healthy dog, so full of bounce, Foxy soon learned, that what counts -
Is the love, that is *all* dogs' right, as she was held and cuddled tight!

She's happy in her nice, new home, this love, before - she'd never known.
They have found a life-long friend, and Foxy's safe, till her life's end!

Joyce Dobson

PUSSYCAT DISGUISE

Black cat - pussycat?
Pussy, my foot!
Black
Little tiger
On my windowsill
Eyeing
My birds!

Frightened birds?

Our two
Curiously bystand
The frantic clawing
On the
Windowpane
Disdaining even
Flight
To their favourite perch
On the light.
They should care!
About a
Black tom,
Bell on collar
Round its neck
Black cat.

Don't they know
The awful
Hunter of the forest
Pays his visit
In pussycat disguise?

Mary Fawbert Wilson

WOODNOTES WILD

Wild animals suggest animals with a savage temperament
Conjuring up, in the mind, quite the wrong sentiment.
Such animals, for the most part, are comparatively mild
And a better definition is: *Those animals which live in the wild.*

Even the human animal can fly into a rage
But no-one suggests, for that, they should be banished to a cage.
Treating all creatures humanely should be the basic key
So that animals in the wild can naturally roam free.

Out on the open range where the mournful buffalo roam,
It may be quite extensive but to them it is their *home.*
To imprison these beasts permanently would be quite absurd
For then they would, most certainly, hear *a discouraging word.*

The lion's a noble beast and, notably, full of pride
But in a circus or zoo cage there *is* nowhere to hide.
When asked to perform unnatural tricks to satisfy adult and child
Is it so surprising that it becomes more *ferocious and wild?*

Russian pandas, with black eyes, in foreign zoos look so cowed.
Is this, perhaps, because they object to mating before a large crowd?
Their refusal to do so may be why they look so glum
But the keepers should thank their good fortune there's not *panda-monium.*

As for eating grandmothers, most wolves are not all that partial!
But, how often are human opinions formed, based on circumstances farcical?
Remember the well-recorded spider which inspired Robert Bruce, by chance?
Now all arachnids are credited with extra powers of perseverance.

So here's strength to the elbow of the WGAS
Which is making giant strides to relieve animals from stress.
Please rally and give your full support, all you generous *guys and gals*
To make life much more comfortable for the *not so dumb* animals.

John W Skepper

189

THE STRIDER

Being older now and in a wiser vein.
I thought a closer friend I should obtain.
This was a dog of collie claim,
whom I thought briefly, would not shame.

From that day forth, I never saw,
the need for loafing, nor the lounging bore.
For we strode miles upon the heath,
chasing rabbit, skylark and any thief.

We thought it splendid fun indeed,
to stride like keepers, at some speed,
through town and countryside so wide.
Till one day we tumbled down and hurt our pride.

From that day on, both man and dog,
decided that to travel, we must jog.
And so it was, we thought best,
to be equipped in shorts and vest.

Not to say, my dog disagreed,
for during worktime, at his own speed.
He tore and rendered my training gear.
Into shreds and pieces, without much fear.

That back to walking, we must proclaim.
As man and beast, friends once again,
that peace with nature, just as before,
and that is really, true friendship's rapport.

Alan Noble

OUR PAL

That small soft bundle we first carried home
has stayed a faithful friend through all the years.
Enjoyed our romps and play when out to roam
and gave us pleasure - chased away our tears.

The fussing of the children when they saw
that tiny tail, pink tongue and whiskery snout.
They loved him when we first came through the door
what fun there was when we all romped about.

The first to wake on mornings and to greet
by dashing up the stairs so craftily.
And then bedclothes pulled from off our feet
and children chased from bedrooms hastily.

His favourite blanket, slipper and his bone
to hide them we all tried but soon he found.
The game he loved to play when on the phone
we had no peace when friends they came around.

If strangers came he soon would let us know
his bark was different and we soon were taught.
By wagging tail or ruffled hairs would show
and so excited when his lead was brought.

We knew like us that he was growing old
now greying whiskers and his slowing trot.
But all that time he trusted us to be
his lifetime pal - he will not be forgot.

Alan J Vincent

ANIMAL REBORN

Viciously, brutally he could not strike dog enough.
Shouting at poor thing in voice harsh and gruff.
Then left it lying a wrecked crumpled ball,
Nearly at life's end, almost past recall.
Someone saw it lying, so with gentle touch,
Laid it in van, saw 'twas hurt so much.
Drove to Wood Green to tell sorry tale,
Was told leave it here we'll help cure his ails.
Dog's frightened eyes told of fear in his heart,
People dressed sores, that was the start,
Teaching him trust, some people were good,
In front of him they placed some nice food.
As he strengthened they took walks each day,
When he got used to it he joined helpers play.
Then to Wood Green came doctor and wife,
Wanting to give animal a friendly life.
Seeing that dog knew he was the one.
Came visiting often till his trust was won.
Once centre was happy dog would have good home.
They allowed doctor to take little chap on.
Then went to see him to know it was there·
That little chap's future was beyond compare.
Past pain behind him dog loves his new home,
A loving and faithful pet now he has grown.
They visit Wood Green to see those special friends,
Without whose ministrations dog's life would have reached end.

Barbara Goode

KIM

The dog next door never makes a sound
She surely is an amazing hound,
She sits in her pen all proper and prim
When I say to her 'Good morning Kim.'

Kim is black and of labrador breed,
She's so obedient, to scold there's no need.
I've never known such a loveable creature
And loyal affection is her very best feature.

With such a nice disposition, it's hard to believe
That a watchdog she'd make, as for that to achieve
Her nature would have to change all around
Then she wouldn't be such a loveable hound.

Kim belongs to the family next door,
A young couple with two girls making four,
They take her for walks across fields and down lanes
And enjoy it immensely except when it rains.

When Kim is inside the house next door
She is always content to lie on the floor
And doesn't create when put out in her pen
For it's only a short while till she's in again.

And so it seems Kim has a happy old life
Without any stress or undue strife,
She deserves all the goodness that comes her way
So we're wishing her happiness day by day.

Gerard Oxley

LET'S TAKE EACH OTHER HOME

My sad eyes study you
Try to look into your soul
Silently I beseech you
Will you take me home

And if you do

Will I be chained, starved, or beaten
So many things I dread

or will we

Run together through meadows and streams
Will I sleep at the foot of your bed

be my master

Let's form a love for each other
Let's bond to one another
Let's take each other home.

Fred Tighe

A SONNET TO TIGGER

She is a feeling and not a presence
With feet so light we merely interface.
Her beauty is a distillèd essence.
She is a thing of delicacy and grace.

Her coat's condition is perfection glowing,
Stripes that match from leg to leg.
Whiskers in broad arcs are bowing
With enormous eyes in a pretty head.

My lady enjoys her ease each morning
Luxuriating on a quilt of down.
She stretches, her legs are stiff and clawing,
She licks a paw and turns around.

At night, this mask slips from her face -
A strange, dangerous feline takes her place.

Nicola Slade

A FRIEND

I heard the patter of tiny paws,
turned my head and there I saw,
a little dog with big brown eyes,
looking so sad I could have cried,
are you lost my little friend,
you have been following me do not pretend,
I am going home to have some tea,
come along you can share with me,
we will ring the station report you lost,
don't look so worried there is no cost,
you could belong to some old dame,
I am calling you dog 'cause I don't know your name,
if no-one claims you I will take you in,
but don't start barking and causing a din,
I will be at work each day,
here at home you must stay,
I'll leave the radio on real low,
to keep you company when I go,
I will walk you when I can,
in the park with my young man,
then you will have another friend,
we will keep you safe to the end.

Teresa Walker

BENNY

Benny do you still remember
Now that you are old and grey
How we went to far off places
For a happy holiday.

Do you still recall the river
Into which you bravely leapt,
And the sunshine on the grassbank
Where dog-dreaming you once slept.

How at first light in the morning
Of a lovely summer's day:
By yourself you went to wander,
Found adventures on your way.

Do you still recall the soft sand
Where you scampered by the sea.
Roamed among the rocks and rock pools -
Brine soaked you came back to me.

Benny have you now forgotten
How we found new secret ways
In the countryside we rambled
On those bygone halcyon days.

Benny! Benny! Stir your slumbers:
Once again the fields to roam,
Just a little way my Benny -
Very soon we'll be back home.

Jack Judd

GUIDE DOG (ANITA)

Her eyes were his
As she led him down the hall
To the piano leaning against the wall.
At his feet she lay
And would stay all day
While her master continued his daily task
To tune the school piano he had been asked
To guard him she would remain
For this,
She had been trained.

Patricia M Farbrother

SHE

She meets me every evening, as I come in the door
She never asks me where I've been, or what I went out for
She lets me know she loves me, in lots of different ways
She never throws a 'tantrum,' no matter what I say
She takes my moods for granted, she never picks a fight
She never says that she's fed up and I am never right
She watches all I'm doing, and never says a word
She knows I would not harm her, or hurt her for the world
She never asks for money, or stares in jewel shops
She'd be the same were I flat broke, or wanted by the cops
She sees me as 'her hero', the nicest of the nice
She doesn't care I've got no hair, and a nose been broken twice
She would walk out with me, if I was dressed in rags
She always is the same with me, I've never heard her nag
She's always tired at bedtime, and lies just like a log
She's not a sexy lover, she's just my little old dog.

Charles Boyett

THE DYING DOLPHIN

I rise and find I can't
I breathe to know I shan't
Entwined and tangled in the nets
Thrashing, lashing, remorse, regrets.

I rode the waves with skill and ease
I skipped the surf on seven seas.
I dived the depths, with wet-backs swam
Then paid the price to fisherman.
To tourists I would gladly glide
The salty tides upon boat side,
A spectacle for all to see
Yet happy, they would seem to be,
So joyous I would stand on tail
Or somersault through frothy veil,
Collecting praises for my game
And then ... become the fisher's shame.
The nets were spread so far and deep
For baby fish the mothers weep
And I, the friend of man and boat
Shall wear the knots for my own coat.

I rise and find I can't,
I breathe to know I shan't,
Entwined and tangled in the nets
Thrashing, lashing, remorse, regrets!

Vince Marsden

MERLIN

The double patio doors were flung open wide.
I remembered one last job and dashed outside,
When I saw him, a young, but fully grown cat.
All white, with black saddle and neat little cap.
I looked at his face, his grape green eyes,
They seemed at once frightened, but infinitely wise.
He had claw marks round his mouth on his muzzle,
How had he got them I started to puzzle?

Then I realised, he'd been fighting for his food,
Being timid, he must have been desperate to do something so crude.
He took nothing for granted, turned, crouched, prepared to go,
I ran inside, grabbed warm chicken and gave it a blow.
Put the bowl down, went indoors and left him alone.
He ate all the meat right down to the bone.
'Twas the beginning of a courtship that lasted two years.
The love story ran on with its share of worries, smiles and tears.

Like the time I had to trap him, to treat a bad wound,
While he suffered the pain and indignity without a sound.
But the trials are over his heart is now won.
He's even weaved his magic on husband, and sons.
When I first found him dirty and so painfully thin,
I wondered, 'Why doesn't God take care of him?'
Then it dawned . . . the Lord did know, he really did see.
He had brought him salvation when he brought him to me.

Linda Miller

BILL

They tell me I'm a sheepdog
With a champion's pedigree
Smooth black with white ruffle,
Handy for the boss to see.

He says 'Come bye,' 'Away now.'
To send me round the flock
But when I try to do my best
They laugh at me and mock.

My mother's famous on TV.
Winner of 'One man and his dog.'
Oh, not for me the call to fame
It's 'Git bye and fetch that hogg.

I've often really wondered
The difference between ewe and tup
What exactly is a gimmer?
In which book can I look it up?

But I think I'm intelligent
As I 'eye' them up again
And let the boss run round the field
And put them in the pen.

For when you come to think of it,
Even though they are his sheep.
An elderly collie just like me
Can't curl up and go to sleep.

It's really quite a cushy life
I've plenty of time to kill
Until the boss shouts at me
'Come here, old lazy Bill.'

M W Richardson

TODAY I LOST A FRIEND

Old Pickles has just died,
and I miss her so much;
I would give anything
to feel again her touch.
For her to lick my hand,
to see her laughing eyes;
hear those excited barks
and her sad doggy sighs.
She was like a shadow
out walking by my side,
sometimes full of mischief
she'd run away and hide;
then peer out craftily
behind a shrub or tree.
She knew my every move,
I seldom had to talk;
she'd race to fetch her lead
the moment I said 'walk.'
I know at times I'd shout
at scratchings on the door;
I'd tell her off as well
at pawmarks on the floor.
If only she were here
to play her tricks again;
and wander in the evening
in meadow field and lane.
She was a loyal friend,
a much loved friend for years;
her picture's here beside me
but blurred because of tears.

David T Wicking

LOVE ALL CREATURES GREAT AND SMALL

Dogs are loveable loyal pets, how I stand and look,
when guide dogs lead their owners in and out of traffic
every clever move, their blind never frets.

Alsations have grace in their movements and loyalty
to the owner, they've rescued people from deep water
they walk out with owner in control, but they still
get complaints from hidden groaners.

Keeping rabbits in hutches seems cruel to me
but they know the people that are kind, they will
eat food out of your hand, and a champion show
rabbit is a real find.

How I love to stand at a fence surrounding
a large expanse of grass, the sight of a horse
frolicking within these grounds when I see one I can
never pass.

Though grey squirrels are considered pests they are
really great to watch, I threw nuts to them at the
bottom of a tree, they were caught. The animal climbed
up the tree to where they build their nests.

David R Price

THE BUZZARD

Soaring, gliding, wheeling, diving,
As all beneath him surveying,
So the hunter prepares to strike
Alas his hunter shoots his like.
No harm to him but he must kill,
Some day to protect you a Bill
King of the clouds, hawk of the skies,
Dive, dive alas no more to rise.

They see that there your body lies
But can they say your spirit dies.
On and on, upwards, always free,
Still the wind brings your call to me.
So heart and soul whichever soars
Can it be captive to their roars.
Man may think the world his decree
He can never own such as thee.

Pippin

SIÂN

I must watch for the sun as it shines
Through the cracks in the door
And if I pray to the God of dogs,
The door might open and I'll be free.
The strangling chain will fall away,
The kicking boots will hurt no more,
The punching fists be stilled.
The ferocious stones stay on the ground
And not be hurled at me.
The shouting and the swearing
Will be silenced.
The quarrelling and the noise
Will be forgotten.
Oh God of dogs, please help me,
Let me feel the wind in my fur,
The rain on my coat, the sun on my face,
Let me be free to run and to play,
Give me a home where I will love
And be loved; will I ever trust a human again?
Oh God of dogs,
How long must I wait,
And count the bars of sunlight
As I watch through the cracks in the door?

Jo Stuart

MAN'S BEST FRIEND

I see the trust in your soft brown eyes,
As you lay at my feet, whilst I am resting,
I feel you relax, let out a deep sigh,
And accept, the love, you now are getting.

It seems a lifetime ago to me,
Since I found you, full of mistrust and fear,
Starving, cold, left tied to a tree,
The thought of it, can still bring a tear.

I took you gently up into my arms,
Talking softly, to try and calm you,
'You're safe now, relax be calm,
I'll take care of you, whatever I do.'

It took an age, to get you well,
To feed you up and make you strong,
To help you, try and forget the hell,
You were put through, when you'd done no wrong

But as time went by, memories started to fade,
You began at long last to trust me,
I knew then, no better choice had I made,
On that day I had set you free

V Woodhouse

PRETEND

Pretend that you're a monkey
A monkey in a zoo,
Look at all those funny faces,
And the antics that they do,
Pretend you're really laughing
And they'll throw nuts to you.

Pretend that you're a penguin
A penguin in a zoo,
Look at all those funny people
And the funny walks they do,
Pretend you've started clapping
And they'll clap back to you.

Pretend that you're an elephant
And elephant in a zoo,
When nosy people stop and stare
You know just what to do,
Pretend you're sniffing water
And they'll stay clear of you.

Pretend that you're a parrot
A parrot in a zoo,
Listen to all their silly talk
It's all people have to do
Pretend you're pretty Polly
And they're all pretty Polly too.

Pretend that you're a lion
A lion in a zoo.
Walk about outside your cage
That's all you have to do,
Pretend you're after dinner
and you'll have an empty zoo.

Peter James O'Rourke

ROBIN REDBREAST

Each day down to the woods I go,
And on the path some crumbs I throw,
There, closely watching from a tree,
A robin redbreast I can see.

He jumps around and chirps away,
A game of hide and seek he'll play.
Then quickly flies down to the ground,
And pecks the crumbs that he has found.

Back swiftly to the tree he flies
To thank me - oh! So hard he tries.
For he just chirps and chirps away,
Then a new game he starts to play.

Loris Quick

FREEDOM

I wanna go where I like
Be whatever I like
Dream whatever I like
Do whatever I like.

I don't wanna be shut away
In the house all day
But to see the countryside
Of woods, birds and animals.

I wanna see the world
Go and discover the universe
Help all the people
And free all the animals.

Juel Duel-Crake

OUR GIFT

Inconspicuous hedgehogs come creeping out at night
From dark places where they hide when it is daylight
They feast on worms and beetles or perhaps a slug or two
Even drink the cats milk that's been left out by you

Badger setts are often found around the countryside
With their paws they dig a hole to breed or just to hide
They eat nice juicy earth-worms or sometimes fallen fruit
Often get run over when folk don't give a hoot

There are many urban foxes in the world today
In parks or in our gardens lots of foxes play
They sometimes feed on squirrels, fallen fruit or a wild bird
Scavenging in dustbins sometimes they are heard

Riding a horse through the green countryside
In the gold gorse-bush the rabbits will hide
A beautiful Bay so free and so wild
Drifting through time like the dreams of a child

Dear little donkeys from Biblical time
Graze in the field where the church bells chime
Friendly, loyal and live to be old
Cousins of the horse I am told

All things living in this world entrusted in our care
Whether fur or feathers fins or silky hair
We have a duty to them all we really must be kind
They are a gift from our dear Lord who we one day shall find

Angela Pearson

THEY ASK FOR SO LITTLE

They don't ask for much just a nice soft bed,
and to have a drink and be well fed,
They don't answer back, and if they don't get a treat
They don't lose their temper and stamp their feet
An encouraging word and a gentle touch
to us seems small, to them means much.
What do they give us in return?
They give us love, when no-one else seems to care,
They are a companion, when there's no-one else there
They are clowns when you're feeling low,
When your down, they are your get up and go,
They are all these things and much, much more.
And all they ask of us, is to be safe and secure.

M Goodwin

A PET LOVING FAMILY

We love all creatures, great and small,
We'd like a giraffe, but it's far too tall.
There are several different kinds of pets in our house,
Though it's out of the question for us to have a mouse.
For we have a beautiful black and white cat,
Which is far less erratic than, say a bat.
Unlike my daughters pet baby rabbit,
Stuck in a hutch he's a creature of habit
The same could be said of our tropical fish
Who all seem somehow to have found their niche,
Our canary sings merrily in his little chrome cage.
Whether he's happy is very hard to gauge.
Finally we have a very large dog
Because I can't imagine me walking a frog!

Michael Boast

208

GIVE ME SHELTER

He was rescued from the cold
found frightened and barely alive
huddled amongst the rubbish
in the refuse tip outside
just another unwanted kitten.

They carried the little bony body
to the safety of their van
and swiftly drive through the night
delivering him to a man
who didn't see just another unwanted kitten.

He and his staff at Wood Green
the Animal Shelter once more had seen
a case such as this unspeakable cruelty
towards just another unwanted kitten.

They nursed the little ginger tom
watched over him night and day
fed him, gave him shelter and a brand new start
so no-one could say
he was just another unwanted kitten.

At six weeks old I saw him
and cuddled this creature now mine,
they gave him to this childless woman
confident in the knowledge that I
through their efforts
now had a wanted kitten.

Marianne Welsh

HOW MANY?

Just think of all the animals
That share the earth with man,
But do you know them all by name?
Count them, if you can.

There's kangaroos and elephants,
There's horses, cows and sheep.
Some can hiss and some can roar
And some don't make a peep.

Some walk, some fly, some crawl along,
And then there's those that jump.
Some have hair and some have fur
And some have got a hump.

And as for colours, black and white,
Yellow, blue or green,
And those that change to suit their mood
Or want to stay unseen.

There's dogs and cats and birds and fish,
There's bears and lizards too,
But do you know how many types
Share the earth with you?

Shirley Mulder

MY PAL - MY DOG!

Who is faithful
Who is true
Who always puts
Their trust in you

They can't speak
or tell you lies
But the look of love
is in their eyes

Those brown eyes
gaze at you
Especially when
lunch is due

They don't ask for much
Just food and drink
To be kept clean
and *off* the streets

The reward you get
is for their lifetime,
A pal, a friend, and
to the lonely and blind
A special *guide line!*

May Read

SNUFFLED

Keeping to the shadows
His swinish snorts resound
Snouting through the undergrowth
A snuffled eerie sound
A hedgehog on a starlit night
Amid the midnight hush
Foraging for food
In the garden's underbrush
Discovering the bread and milk
I've left him on a plate
He scuttles off excitedly
His good news to relate
Returning soon with family
They tuck in to his find
Then startled, curl up into balls
As I creep up behind
Defensive spiky creatures
That my presence has alarmed
Displaying prickly suits
With which they have all been armed
I move away and listen
As, relaxing once again,
Their snuffled chorus drowns
The restless grasshoppers' refrains.

Kim Montia

JOURNEY OF AN OTTER

Crescent shaped nostrils disguise valves within,
Holding back a deep breath before gliding in,
Trapped warm air inside a fur like skin,
Streamlined trunk designed for swimming,
Propelled forwards by a long muscular tail,
Only surface bubbles marking the watery trail.

An inquisitive nature spies a river bed,
Turning stone with five toe nails, webbed,
Through murky depth of dense vegetation,
Sensitive whiskers search the vibrations,
Snatching a prized eel in a moments turbulence,
A feast leading towards a watery entrance.

Sense guiding through the tunnel of dark night,
Seeking the comforting holt and subdue light,
Pausing for rest until arising to a view,
Trails of musky spraints marks horizons new,
Characteristics pose, a method known as tripoding,
Looks of elevation whilst instincts sense foreboding.

A sloped embankment follows a jelly like spray,
Indulging on occasional amphibians along the way,
With flexing motions plays upon a muddy slide,
Paddling in shallow depth tossing pebbles aside,
Dextrous forepaws tumbles with a ball of stone,
The journey ends safely at a second watery home.

Kathleen Speed

MUTT

He lies there waiting at his master's gate
Shaggy ears drooping as he waits
for him he loves so well.

At each new noise his hedgerow eyebrows rise
and fall to hide the amber eyes,
sad in lonely vigil.

Patiently he trembles there as he lies.
His nostrils quiver as he sighs.
Cold his licorice nose.

Heavy paws lightly rest on the roughness
of his shingle couch as he lies.
His heavy jaws set firm.

The warm sun softly shines and stirs aflame;
as he ponders this waiting game,
and glosses his rough coat.

His aching heart will not be faint at all
until he hears anew the foot fall
of him he loves so well.

Elizabeth Goffin

LIFE ON EARTH

Life on earth is oft not blessed
With babies smile or family nest,
Then oft do our attentions seek
With furry friends who cannot speak.

Love pours out on placid hound
Who cannot in this life astound
Us by his talk and speech of thanks
They only walk in animal ranks.

But when to heaven we shall ascend
And to our glorious Lord attend,
His blessings all will us surround
And life be joyful and new found.

God's special children wait for you
With paws outstretched and love anew
There the silent cat so sleek
There in Heaven the dumb shall speak.

Jean Carroll

THEIR LAST HOME RUN

A tanker ran aground that stormy night
Spilling tons of oil in the dull evening light.
The crew were winched to safety for all to see
For what was to unfold was an environmental and wildlife tragedy.

The water was black, as black as coal
Thick with oil gushing from the ship's ruptured hull.
'What's happened, has happened,' I heard a distant cry.
I couldn't believe what was said, when so many creatures would die.

Like tar the oil stuck to the beach
Leaving so many seabirds out of reach.
I felt so helpless knowing what should have been done
And if only that oil tanker had never come.

The next day I walked along the blackened shore
Where silver coloured fish were dead. A thousand or more.
Like oily rags, sea birds lay dying in the sun.
For many a gull or cormorant it was their last home run.

Rod Stalham

A MOTHER'S PAIN

Three times I've been pregnant
Each time my babies die
And not through natural causes
But it's *man* that makes me cry.

Every time I've given birth
My cub was cute and strong,
Each time I fed it lovingly
But it never lasted long.

The men all come with clubs in hand
To bash my baby's head,
I tried to fight, got hurt myself
Too late, my baby's dead.

The pain in my breast is
From unwanted milk,
There are cuts and dried blood
On my coat smooth as silk.

I'm pregnant again
And this time I will try,
But I need man to help
Or my baby will die.

C A Prior

MY LITTLE PUPPY

I have a little puppy, he's as mischievous as can be,
He chews up all the furniture, and comes chasing after me.
He barks and he yelps, and he scratches at the door,
He tears up bits of paper and scatters it on the floor.
He chews up shoes and slippers, anything in his way,
I love my little puppy, I got him yesterday.

Carol Tibbles

BEASTFULLY YOURS!

My dear master, I must write
(As I lie on the floor),
I think it's time to rearrange
This *man and dog* rapport.
You see, although I love you
And I'm told I'm your best friend,
I feel some things need changing
And the household rules must bend . . .
For starters, I get ruffled
When you tell me not to bark
So, in return for hush -
An extra hour in the park!
I also want more Squeakies
And I'd like a double feed -
A tartan coat and collar
And a brand new leather lead.
Two pairs of fur-lined slippers
Just to central heat my paws,
And weekly visits to the vets
To manicure my claws!
A special place upon the couch
That I can call my own,
And also by the fire -
With a lavish daily bone!
A bath when I request it -
And no truces with the cat,
And extra-special fussing -
Is it not too much to ask?

So now I've written down my laws,
Dear Master (yap!) Beastfully Yours!

Lynda Ann Green

MASTER'S MOODS

I basked one night before the fire
Snug on master's knees:
All that is a dog's desire
And my attempt to please.

The look upon the master's face
Suggested thoughts divine;
He stroked my ears in silence . . .
'Til the clock began to chime.

The situation, now transformed
He jumped up, most perturbed;
Pitched my off towards the rug
And thus my confidence disturbed.

I hurried to my basket
As things began to fly,
When master couldn't find his hat;
(I knew he'd do so, by and by)

After all, I'd only borrowed it
With things a little dull
To chew the brim and worry it,
(Now that was really fun).

I waited on the staircase
For master to return;
I'd hoped to be forgiven
And no longer to be spurned.

I gave him my angelic look
When he finally appeared,
For I wanted him to love me . . . as
Before his hate had disappeared!

I had no need to worry
For now I had a bone;
Took master for a walk and thus
for my sins atoned.

Ted Herbert

MY DOG LOUIS

Farewell loyal friend, sleep well
free from pain,
I can't believe I won't see
you again.
You've left an emptiness, a void
in my life,
A pain in my heart that cuts
like a knife.
You gave so much pleasure
over the years,
Now you are gone and
left only tears,
But life goes on, and I look
back with love.
And hope you're looking down
from above.
There will always be room
in my heart for you,
My confidante, my friend
so true.

Y M Powell

MY FRIEND ROVER

I want a puppy screamed my son
His sisters joined in too

We'll feed and walk him every day
We won't leave it all to you

Like a fool I nodded my head
With me they could always get round

They squealed with joy and utter delight
As we entered the lost and found

They finally picked the dog for them
A shabby looking cur

It only looked a few weeks old
With tatty long brown hair

'It's your turn to walk him,' the girls would shout
My son would look in dismay

'That's not fair I've walked him once
And twice round the block yesterday'

As they got older, new interests they had
Rover's walks were now left to me

But I didn't mind, no not at all
I'd grown fond of him too you see

Soon they were married with kids of their own
And sometime would all come over

Their kids would play and make a fuss
Of now a near blind Rover

He's getting rather old now
And at my feet he does lie

He has become my one good friend
And I pray don't let him die!

Pamela Harrison

DIVIDED LOVE

It's late, and he sits near me,
Love shines in his eyes,
He knows I wait for someone else,
We have no need for lies.

He needs no explanations,
He knows my love, he'll share,
He never asks for anything,
Just tender loving care.

Tonight, we sit in silence,
We've nothing else to do,
He'll stay in vigil at my side,
His love, for me stays true.

I gently reach to touch him,
He shivers in the dark,
Then the silence of the *waiting game*
Is shattered by his bark.

He stands to the sound of his master's keys
As he comes through the door,
His duties done, he wags his tail,
And goes to sleep once more.

Jayne Jenkins

CARE FOR OUR CREATURES

We should all remember
God put us all on earth,
Humans, creatures, nature too,
He gave all life their birth,
Why do we think we have the right,
To torture, kill and maim,
These lesser creatures of our earth,
For truly we all came,
From the very source above,
And brought to earth to live,
So stop this torture and this pain,
To our creatures that we give,
Cosmetics tested on them,
With horrible results,
Snares and traps for animals,
These tortures kept occult,
Driftnets killing dolphins,
Killing whales as well,
Sealing culls should just be banned,
It is a living hell,
Veal calves being reared in crates,
Hounds that hunt for pleasure,
Man is just responsible,
Our creatures we should treasure,
Please just help us all you can,
By supporting us all round,
With petitions for the Governments,
Our cause is justly found,
So think about the things you buy,
Don't encourage this bad way,
Help our defenceless creatures,
Along their life's pathway.

Janette Campbell

NEVER TO GROW OLD

I suck my first milk straight away
But then my poor mum was taken away
I am shoved and I am pushed into a large van
With others like me we all cry for our mums

Then we are pushed into a large ring
With people all around us and bidding begins
The noise and the shouting are making us scared
We are loaded onto a lorry in three or four pairs

We travelled all night and morning as well
Then we are let out into a place we call hell
I am pushed into a box with a chain around my neck
And fed from a bucket with milk I can only just get

I try to turn around but find I cannot move
I pine for my mum as I struggle and pull
Everyday I am stuck inside this small crate
My legs I cannot stretch my body so aches

As I grow bigger there is less room to move
I heard that man saying this one for the kill
I am carted around to yet another place
Where animals are all crying my heart starts to race

I follow the calves up to a blue gate
We are shaking with fear at the smell of our fate
Next in the line I am waiting with fear
Then the big bang that's the last thing I hear.

Susan Davies

THE MOUSE

We heard a little noise when lying in our bed
A scratching and a rustling. It came from overhead.

We've got another a mouse. It's happened once again.
They come inside in winter. It's really such a pain.

We had a mouse last Christmas, which terrified our hound,
ate all her doggie biscuits. Really quite a mound.

We had to catch this creature our dog had grown quite thin,
kept hiding under the table, whenever the mouse came in.

We bought a little trap - you know the kindly kind,
it doesn't hurt the mouse and we baited it with rind.

We caught the little blighter, quite quickly I'm glad to say
and carried it to the fields about half a mile away.

But to our great annoyance this clever little chap,
arrived back that very same evening, didn't even have a map.

We knew about his visit when the dog began to quake
and quite a chunk went missing from our uncut Christmas cake.

Again we caught Houdini, by now this was his name
and took him to the railway and put him on a train.

He reached Victoria Station with only two hours delay
and we received a postcard, which arrived unstamped next day.

'I've found a plastic beaker, which really is quite nice,
it provides a cosy shelter for us vagrant little mice.

The food here is quite tasty, I dine well every day
on hundreds of BR sandwiches, which humans have thrown away.

They accidentally drop them whilst running for their train.
It really is quite careless, but their loss is my gain.

The sandwiches leave craters in the platform when they fall.
It can get quite dangerous, 'cos us little folk aren't tall.

But if a female of my species should gain access to your house,
I'm feeling a trifle lonely and would like to have a spouse.'

Pauline Brennan

CANDY

Our cat Candy is dead
I'll bury her straight away
In the corner of the garden
Where she used to play

I chose a likely spot
And busied with my spade
Where she could lay undisturbed
No better place was made

I dug away blindly
As the tears ran down my cheeks
I can't believe it's happened
Although she's been ill for weeks

Her favourite teddy bear
With which she used to sleep
I placed alongside her
In the grave so deep

I said a little prayer
As I shovelled back the earth
And thanked her for the joy she brought
Every second's worth.

K Coleman

A WICKED OLD CAT

A wicked old cat from Cardiff Bay
Grabbed his belongings and was on his way
A world of adventure he intended to seek
With excitement to find on every street
He dodged in and out of traffic galore
Painstaking steps with every paw
His valour not dimmed as he struggled and fought
To reason with traffic that hadn't a thought
For a wicked old cat who adventures rang true
Longing to find all new things to do
New to the motorway, its pace no thrill
May lead to an adventure of speed or kill
Don't be silly old cat, just hurry home
To your loving family, your basket so warm
You're our own family pet with that wicked way
Which we'll love and adore till your dying day
Hurry home, your mischief done
We'll keep an eye on you, from now on
Safely does it, step by step
Home once more with no regrets.

Irene Pearce

ONE LAST CALL

Brown velvet eyes appealing for pity
Melt aching heart and turn knees to jelly
'What can I do?' I cry,
But there's no reply.

Breathing erratic as spasms return
Forehead and nose feel so hot my hand burns.
'I love you!' I cry,
Again no reply.

Bravely he watches me go down the hall
Pick up the phone and make that last call
'He can't walk!' I cry,
And dread the reply.

Brown velvet eyes, relieved of their pain
Flicker, just once as tears flood mine again.
'End of line,' I cry
As my gentle giant dies.

Betty Lightfoot

MY BEST FRIEND

My best friend, he's got fleas,
And they do tend to tease,
But I told him don't despair,
Fleas they only like clean hair,
But my mum did not agree,
As she was bitten by a flea,
Oh. she was so full of woe,
And down the plughole the fleas did go.
She washed them off with a special shampoo,
That looked suspiciously like glue,
And now my friend does scratch no more,
And I find it quite a bore,
But if I take him out to play,
I'm sure another will jump his way,
You see they are attracted to his furry coat,
What a strange friend I hear you gloat,
Well your memory here I'd like to jog,
My best friend - he is a dog.

J M Habgood

GIVE ME A CHANCE
(A mistreated horse's life in India)

One more lash and I am down
My mind lifts and jumps and flies,
To an untouched paradise
Where no hand will hurt me anymore,
The cries of sorrow will disappear
And my heart will not cry with pain
No more.
Dragged to my feet, all hurts and pains
People will laugh as I hurt, so much more
I could almost sob, but no sound shall come
As God takes a hand,
And I am gone.

Melissa Sherwood

MY POEM

A dog is known as a man's best friend
who'll follow you right until the end,
so feed him well and give him care
to treat him wrong is just not fair.
A cat is loving, soft and nice
by day it sleeps
at night hunts mice,
she snuggles down and starts to purr
and lets you tickle her clean fur
A fish needs a tank with lots of room
for a horse you need a brush to groom
A rabbit needs a hutch, kept clean
feed your pets well and don't be mean

Michelle Fuller (11)

228

SAM

My best friend was only
one foot tall
He was born early spring
As mother nature made her call
He'd a coat of satin, colours
of a rusty hue,
A stumpy tail, constantly barked
I'll give you a clue.
His breed rhymes with bustle
Yes you've guessed it's a Jack Russell.

It only seems like yesterday, we
Walked and made our way
Down to the meadow where
Sam would join us children
In rough and tumble play
Through all kinds of weather
The wind, sun and rain, a cut, mucky
hands, we had such fun
And tired were we at the
close of day.

Sam, though you're just a memory
Visions of you time to time
I see
You were cute, so full of energy
Now in heaven above
Reborn and free
I'm sure you still remember me

Margaret Jowsey

CONCRETE EARTH

The flowers have all gone
And where are the bees
There's a big concrete road
They've cut down the trees.

The land has all changed
They've altered the features
I'm glad that I'm not one of
God's little creatures.

So where are the sounds
Of the birds melodies
There's no more dawn chorus
Cos' there isn't any trees

There's nowhere to wander
Only a flat solid state
Now it's dangerous to move
And there's nowhere to mate.

So will they all die
And it will be a shame
Now the roads taken over
It'll never be the same.

We're killing the land
Of our beautiful earth
So why do we do it
And what's it all worth.

So stop building more roads
Let the animals roam free
Leave the woodlands alone
And look after the tree.

David Brownley

GONE

Gone the lemmings to the sea,
honey from a bee.

Ducks flying by,
a plane in the sky.

A fox to its lair,
a speeding hare.

A galloping horse,
a rabbit on its course.

Hounds on the scent,
Those on foot, as they went.

A river speeding by,
the antics of a fly.

A leaping frog,
a sleeping dog.

A badger down its hole
a disappearing mole.

Leaves from a tree,
a cake for tea.

A racing car
a falling star.

A passing train,
an injury, pain.

All gone, like our love.

Margaret Cave

MY NEW HOME

I had a home a while ago,
but my owners moved away
they said we do not want you,
now, so I became a stray,
it was so cold and miserable, but
thought I must not mope,
Just carried on as best I could
and didn't give up hope,
One day a kindly neighbour
who noticed my distress, said
do come in, I must have looked
a mess, there's food and drink a
nice warm bed, so settle by the
fire, please stay with me, I'm
on my own, we'll both have
company, I am so very happy
there, much better than the past,
It couldn't be more purr-fect
cause I'm really safe at last

J Kempton

ANIMAL LOVE

Animals are loving
Animals are kind
Animals seem to be so much
better than mankind

Animals are trusting,
and don't ask for much.
All they seem to ask
is food and water;
humans' demands aren't
as such.

Little piggies are much better
than us humans;
with their cute, nosy
pink snout!
So, tomorrow, I'm off
to buy me a piggie, and
I'm kicking my boyfriend out!

Dawn Christy

A THOUGHT FOR A HEDGEHOG

Did you feel my pain,
did you shed a tear.
That night in the rain
did you think I was dear.

I didn't have a chance,
in your headlight trance.

A second for life,
a second for death,
Away in the night,
there I was left.

Does anybody feel,
does anybody care,
I'm a motionless nothing,
in the cold night air.

You're tucked up snug
in your cosy abode,
I'm your prickly friend,
you left squashed in the road.

N Cantelo

A MESSY LASS

Come on please it's 8am
I need to go outside
you get my lead
I will guard your coat
Then we will walk together, side by side
My big brown eyes look up to you
with love and adoration
I really don't ask for much.
Perhaps just a little consideration
I chase the cats
and bark at ducks
and wag my tail with glee.
When all the children gather around
to make a fuss of me.
A muddy pool upon the bank
I think I will have a splash
Masters always telling me that
I'm such a messy lass
My lead is now between my teeth
homebound we must go
Into the warmth of a cosy place
to have kisses rained upon my face
My nose it glistens my eyes
are so bright. My master tells all
'Her coat is a beautiful sight.'
I will stay with him for evermore
and bark really loud
When someone knocks our door

Lesley Haslett

SEAGULLS' RUNWAY

I tip my butt
And dip my beak,
My winds a'spread
I downward peak.

The scales of fish,
My landing lights,
That guide me on
In downward flights.

The wind blows flat
Upon the sea,
To make my runway
Clear and free.

The parting foam
Plots out the line,
That landing strip,
This sea of mine.

I glide my feet
Along the top,
No breaks to help me
Gently stop.

All kinds of birds
Will come and go
No human eye
Shall ever know.

Then as by magic
All is gone,
So I may fish
And sail along

J Byrne

ALL CREATURES GREAT AND SMALL

The elephant, the hippo too,
The tall giraffe, the kangaroo,
Koala bears and friendly apes -
All different sizes, different shapes,
The doggie world, with various breeds,
The many cats, with many needs,
Massive eagles -soaring heights,
Tiny wrens, with smaller flights,
Field mice, dormice, rarely seen,
Scurrying through the pastures green,
The massive creature, tiny mite,
All precious in their Maker's sight.

Jean M Beavan

THE MOVE

At last I have got my very own home;
they've given my bed, bowls and a bone.
I'm nervous, you see, fresh from the pound
and its awfully quiet here, no others around.

I like my box; it's under the stairs,
So they won't creep up on me unawares.
I've a big bowl for water, and another for food,
With plenty of toys for when play is my mood.

The children seem like nice gentle guys,
they look through the banisters, big puppy dog eyes.
I think that this house will suit me quite well.
I'm sure that they'll love me, a stray dog can tell.

A M Barwani

HARRY THORNLEY

My name is Keith, not postman Pat
But all the same I have a black and white cat.
He follows me here, he follows me there
Yes, Harry, my cat, follows me everywhere.

Often when doing my paper round
I will hear that familiar me-ow-ing sound.
And if I post a letter, which never takes long,
I still hear Harry bounding along.

But when I reach a busy road
Harry will go into 'stationary mode'
He'll not go home, just sit and wait
Perhaps behind a bush or a garden gate.

Then on my way home he'll dash under my feet
Could be waiting for me is his special treat.
Sometimes he'll wait till I'm yards and yards past
Then thunder along till he's caught up at last.

And when he goes out late at night
He keeps very low and out of sight
Then just when I think it's time for bed
The cat-flap will click and I'll see a familiar head.

He'll dart straight for the window and sit in his stool
Just to check things once more - he's nobody fool.
Then when he's content that everything's alright
He'll curl up on my lap
And if it was up to Harry
He'd stay there all night.

Keith Thornley ·

A FAMILY'S GAIN

Lulu,
That was her name,
Of the dog that became ours,
But 'twas such a shame,
Of the way she had been treated,
Before becoming our gain.

Into our family, firstly she came,
From the RSPCA to grandparents,
Who gave her a name,
For before she was nothing
Shut in the door,
Used like an ashtray,
Kicked around the floor.

Cared for by grandparent
By night and by day,
For Lulu, their little 'waif and stray,'
Then when the time came, we were
given her too,
And gave her a home,
A comfortable bed (or two!)

I still think of the day,
When I was still a boy,
When Lulu came to stay,
And gave us so much joy.

The sadness that was felt,
The day Lulu did not wake up,
To a dog that meant so much,
God bless you, farewell.

Ian Bromidge

ANGELS IN FUR COATS

Whenever I open my window,
I'm blest by the gentle purr,
from two special angels in disguise;
wearing glossy coats of fur:

These heavenly, feline creatures
give me hours, of sheer delight:
for one of them, is white, with black:
and the other, black with white.

They came, from an animal shelter
and I've loved them, right from the start:
A mother cat, with her baby.
Who tugs at the strings of my heart

Reclining near my window,
they enhance the rural scene.
And two pairs of eyes, observe me
which are, a dusky green.

I offer them, light refreshment:
it's the least, that I can do.
I open up my window,
and pass two saucers, through.

Their frequent visits, I treasure;
so their mission, they clearly fulfill:
And I couldn't wish, for a sweeter disguise
to grace my window sill.

I anoint them with my blessing:
(So cute, and free from sin)
For being my companions,
on the outside looking in:

P Gross

FRIEND

Child like gaze and the depth of halcyon
                              in your eyes,
Somehow a feeling of joy that never dies.
The windows of your soul baying to stygian
                              clouds of crescent moon,
Lignite coat in the distance scuds past
                              the sidereal lit lagoon.
Hours and days, it seems we were last together,
Never once did you forget even in clement weather.
For when we last parted, you never
                              stopped to say goodbye,
I know you will return, I just have to sigh.
Reminiscence of you and me when we
                              were both small,
Fondness for each other becomes a total recall.
By the fireside you slept next to me
                              without a care,
Sublime dreams of each other in
                              silent night air.
For a long time we have been close,
                              this is my monologue,
Man's best friend you truly are, you're my orb,
                              you're my dog.

John Watson

WHITE (SAMOYED) HAIRS EVERYWHERE

Just one scratch, that's all it takes
For a single hair to float away
And when or where it lands may be
A guessing game for several days.

They flutter into everything
At washing time when things are clean
And from there into every drawer
To settle silently, unseen.

You find them all about the house
Those little silver-white offenders
Hiding in the smallest places
Amongst your socks and red suspenders.

You brush the stray from off the table
Cutlery and salad bowl
But when it comes to dinner time
There's one right in your casserole.

You stand back from your decorating
So pleased that everything is new
And when the paint has nearly dried
You spot one on your woodwork too!

They're even on the Scrabble board
Inside that book you've almost read,
Sometimes in your cup of tea,
On granny's teeth beside her bed.

We love our dogs, their hair and all
Although it means we're never free
Of hairless surfaces and things
Without our Sams, where would we be!

Sarah Ropella

INFORMATION

We hope you have enjoyed reading this book - and that you will continue to enjoy it in the coming years.

If you like reading and writing poetry drop us a line, or give us a call, and we'll send you a free information pack.

Write to

Anchor Books Information
1-2 Wainman Road
Woodston
Peterborough
PE2 7BU